Awaken Your CAI

A HOLISTIC ROAD MAP TO CLIMB FROM YOUR CALLING TO YOUR CAREER
by Alexia Vernon

"Now you have the perfect guidebook to help you live your purpose and create more abundance (on the inside and out) each day of your life. Awaken Your CAREERpreneur will unleash your entrepreneurial spirit and jumpstart your life in a whole new direction."

Gabrielle Bernstein, Author, Add More ~ing to Your Life: A Hip Guide to Happiness, Founder, HerFuture.com, Speaker

"With Awaken Your CAREERpreneur, career expert and coach Alexia Vernon offers a series of practical and creative exercises and questions for reflection that both encourage and challenge change-seekers to identify a path based on their unique gifts and core values, and to embark on a career journey that is based on authenticity. While GenY-ers will especially appreciate Vernon's voice, the less technologically-adept will also find useful tips to help take the fear out of essential career growth and networking strategies such as personal branding and maximizing social media resources."

Jennifer Fishberg, Author of FabJob.com's Become a Career Coach

"Alexia finds a way to simplify the ability to strengthen one's weaknesses while promoting one's strengths. Job seekers or individuals who want to achieve their career goals should read Awaken Your CAREERpreneur before they begin the grueling job search."

Chelsey Kuzyk, Associate Director of Career Services, DeVry University

"I love Alexia Vernon's Awaken Your CAREERpreneur! It is so practical and yet motivational. Having the worksheets makes readers more likely to fill things out right then and there enabling them to get even more out of the book as they progress through it. My favorite part is the Building Your Network section, but I also really love the idea of creating a vision board with the offer letter to the company of my choice."

Sue Stephenson, MPA, CPRW, CEIP, Career Coach and Counselor, Utah Valley University

"In Awaken Your CAREERpreneur, Alexia Vernon's advice packs a punch and guides you as you define your brand and push forward in your career to make an indelible mark."

Vicki Salemi, Author, Big Career in the Big City, Speaker, Former Recruiting Executive

Awaken Your CAREERpreneur

A HOLISTIC ROAD MAP TO CLIMB FROM YOUR CALLING TO YOUR CAREER

by Alexia Vernon

Disclaimer:

While the publisher and author have taken proper precautions to ensure that all of the information provided is factually accurate, errors and omission may still exist. Be mindful of this when making choices about your career and always follow your own best judgment or seek professional counsel before taking action.

Published by:

Joshua Tree Publishing   Chicago   JoshuaTreePublishing.com

All rights reserved. No part of this book may be reproduced or transmitted in any form or by any means, electronic or mechanical, including photocopying, recording or by any information storage and retrieval system without written permission from the author or publisher.

Joshua Tree Publishing books are available at special quantity discounts to use for sales promotions, employee premiums, or educational purposes. Please e-mail our Order Department to order or for more information at:

order@joshuatreepublishing.com

For Allen, the Ultimate CAREERpreneur
Thank you for modeling how to live with passion, dignity and
resilience. Your legacy is one to be proud of.

Dear Natalie,
I can't wait to
see what you "awaken"
next. So happy to
re-connect again.
Warmly,
Alexia

Awaken Your CAREERpreneur

A HOLISTIC ROAD MAP TO CLIMB FROM YOUR CALLING TO YOUR CAREER

TABLE OF CONTENTS

Foreword

By Gabrielle Bernstein

I first met Alexia Vernon in Spring 2009 when I was asked to be her mentor through the Step Up Women's Network. The ladies at Step Up were thrilled to match us because they saw that we would be the perfect fit. I'm a speaker, coach and self-help book author—Alexia, a speaker, coach, trainer and aspiring author, hence the awesome mentor/mentee match up. I too was excited with this pairing the moment I read Alexia's bio. I nearly fell off my seat when I learned what she'd accomplished. By the time she was 28, she was already a coach certified through the International Coach Federation (ICF), had launched her own career and leadership coaching company, Catalyst for Action, spoke at organizations like the National Association of REALTORS® and National Council for Workforce Education, and at the time also managed to teach public speaking, theatre, and women's studies for local universities. After reading these credentials I thought, *"Wow, she should be mentoring me!"*

When we met it was CAREERpreneur love at first sight! From my very first conversation with Alexia, I knew this was a woman on a powerful mission. She wanted to design a platform that would support the entrepreneurial spirit within us all. Alexia believed you didn't have to be working for yourself to nurture your inner entrepreneur and wanted the world to know this. She was willing to do whatever it took to give birth to this miraculous offering. I'm pleased to say, with *Awaken Your CAREERpreneur*, she has done it!

The timing for this book couldn't be better. Today we must think without a box to create abundant possibilities and, as Alexia will share with you in the pages to come, recognize that *"career success is our birthright."* I can speak with authority on this topic, as I am a serial entrepreneur who started her first two businesses at twenty-one, published two books by thirty and most importantly, created the life of my dreams. Now more than ever, we have an infinite capacity to let our entrepreneurial spirit shine. In fact, we have to. In order to stimulate the economy, feel abundant and love our lives, and use our gifts to positively impact others, we must be creative and fearless. And now you have the perfect guidebook to help you live your purpose and create more abundance (on the inside and out) each day of your life.

Awaken Your CAREERpreneur will unleash your entrepreneurial spirit and jumpstart your life in a whole new direction. You'll be guided to cultivate the primary tools for CAREERpreneurship through Alexia's fun and effective best practices for developing the mindset, relationships, skills, and materials to make career success a way of *being*. In each chapter, Alexia will share her practical advice, real-world examples, and her delicious SUCCESSwork recipes to ensure that you are able to take what you read, implement it, and achieve the results you desire.

I'm proud to introduce you to this guidebook for career success and the brilliant woman who will lead you on your way. Enjoy your journey with Alexia and *Awaken Your CAREERpreneur*!

—Gabrielle Bernstein,
Speaker/Author *of Add More ~ing To Your Life: A Hip Guide to Happiness/*
Founder of HerFuture.com

Introduction

Are you yearning to connect who you are with what you do and derive greater life satisfaction and financial abundance?

Are you looking for innovative strategies to stand out in today's competitive marketplace?

Do you want to learn how to build and sustain a successful career as our nation transitions into a green economy?

If you answered YES to one or more of the questions above, keep reading. I have written *Awaken Your CAREERpreneur* for you!

The idea for this book has been building inside of me since I began my own journey to shift from seeing myself as a serial employee to a CAREERpreneur. When my partner of five years asked, *"Will you marry me?"* I realized that although I could answer his somewhat rhetorical question, I didn't yet have an answer to my own more pressing one, *"Who do I want to be by the time I get married?"* I loved the company I had been working for, and yet I felt like I had reached a bit of a professional dead end. While I felt jazzed when advising our participants on their academic and career plans and when leading a variety of educational trainings, this was becoming an increasingly smaller part of my management role. I couldn't shake the feeling that I wasn't playing to my strengths and enthusiasms as much as I wanted or deserved to be. Furthermore, I owed more in student loan money than I was making in a year. And on the nonprofit salary I earned at the time, that reality was not going to abate any time soon.

My search for how to better align my calling with my career jumpstarted a process of self-discovery that culminated with me studying to be a coach, getting certified through the International Coach Federation (ICF), teaching communication, women's studies, and theatre for local universities, and launching my own career and leadership coaching company, Catalyst for Action, to empower leaders across industries and sectors to build careers and companies to achieve what I call the 3 S's: success, sustainability, and a positive social impact. Most importantly, by the time I said, *"I do,"* barefoot on the beach in Kauai, I had learned to stop making choices out of fear and familiarity. I eliminated my often times unproductive and self-sabotaging thoughts, feelings, and behaviors by creating a new habit of approaching my choices with courage, clarity, and compassion.

As the daughter of a helping professional and serial entrepreneur, I always yearned to fuse my desires to make a difference and a living. While in college I had no qualms about writing my own guidebook for how to make this happen. I started my own nonprofit girls' leadership institute and honed my teaching skills and supplemented my salary by teaching dance for a local ballet company. By the time I finished college and graduate school, however, I had created a dichotomy between impact and profit. And feeling more motivated by the former, I embarked on a succession of j-o-bs. By the time I got married, I had held just over ten post high-school jobs — sometimes as many as four at one time!

According to the Bureau of Labor Statistics (BLS), I was in good company. The BLS guesstimates that Millennials or Generation Y — my 80-95 million member generation born between 1978-2000 — will have approximately 9 jobs between ages 18-32. Other experts like Mark Heckler, President of Valaparaiso University, predict that 17-22 year olds will change jobs an average of 30 times over their careers. Regardless of which expert(s) ultimately have the correct number for my rising generation, two things are for certain. One, unlike our Baby Boomer parents who the BLS says will have held between 10-11 jobs throughout their careers, career change for us really is not change at all. It is a cornerstone of our career trajectory. And two, professionals irrespective of age must re-envision the way we think about and craft our careers to engineer and sustain success in a culture of incessant employee movement. All of us must shift from thinking of ourselves as employees, or even business owners, to CAREERpreneurs.

Entrepreneurs drive innovation in business, lead its start-up, and assume its risk. CAREERpreneurs are people who drive innovation in our careers by connecting our values, strengths, resources, and enthusiasms to opportunities in the marketplace so that we can make an impact and a profit. Just like entrepreneurs, CAREERpreneurs are very clear on what we bring to the table, know how to share who we are and the solutions we can deliver in an irresistible way to a prospective audience, and believe wholeheartedly that success is in our hands and cultivated through keen choices in thinking, believing, and behaving. Sometimes CAREERpreneurs take a position with a company. Other times we consult with multiple organizations or start our own business. With increasing frequency, CAREERpreneurs dance a little bit between all three. CAREERpreneurship is not about medium; it's about mindset and process.

In the following chapters, you will have the opportunity to ignite your own CAREERpreneur and share him or her with those who need him or her most—whether you are about to graduate from school, make a career transition, or simply want to identify your two-steps ahead to create and manifest for yourself the opportunities that let you live your passion.

The book is designed for those who have a sense of what they would like to be doing professionally and know that they need some cheerleading and structure to get there. My hope is that you read and complete one chapter each week over the next four months, giving you ample time to understand, compile, and experiment with the myriad tools necessary to grow a successful career. While you can of course read the book at whatever speed you like, give yourself the gift of completing each chapter's SUCCESSwork (practical exercises for you to move from theory to action) at the time you read the chapter to ensure that the material gets out of your head and into practice.

The weekly, sequential SUCCESSwork will take a variety of forms. At the beginning, you will learn how to replace limiting thoughts, beliefs, and behaviors with nourishing ones, creating the mindset necessary for sustainable career success. In other chapters, you will work on developing skills; for example, you will learn how to use online social media for career building and to articulate verbally and in your professional materials (e.g., Paragraphs of Introduction, cover letters, and resumes) the unique benefits you can deliver. In each chapter you will have opportunities to connect the professional with the personal, such as when you identify your All-Star Team or create your rehearsal script for informational and traditional interviews.

Now, before we embark on our journey together, I want to leave you with the following tips for enabling your success.

10 Ways to Get the Most Out of *Awaken Your CAREERpreneur*

1. Focus on *who* you want to be now and throughout your career and not just on *what* you want to do or *what* you want to achieve. While having goals are important, CAREERpreneurs make space for possibilities by letting go of attachment to particular outcomes.

2. Remember that to learn, grow, and achieve we must be open to trying new ways of thinking, feeling, and behaving. Sometimes that is going to feel uncomfortable, and that is a-okay! We do our best work when pushed slightly outside of our comfort zone.

3. Share who you are, what you want, and how you can provide value with everyone you encounter. CAREERpreneurship works best when you get out from behind a computer screen, take smart and bold action, and connect with other people.

4. Forgive yourself and others for what has happened in the past. Reframe mistakes as opportunities to reflect on what has happened and reapply what you have learned as you bulldoze forward.

5. Keep a possibility-centered mindset. If you experience fear, self-doubt, or apathy setting in, remind yourself, "If you think it, it just might happen." What are the thoughts you want to be putting out into the world? Focus on forming and replaying them!

6.   Get out of your own way. I will support you to identify and replace unproductive habits with more nutritious, success-inducing ones. Resist the temptation to think anything is permanent just because it is a familiar or long-lasting way of being. *(As you will learn in Chapter 2, it takes just over 90 days to create a new habit).*

7.   Live a healthy lifestyle. As my yoga teacher Sherry Goldstein says, *"If you don't take care of your body, you have no place to live."* Make sure that you are getting enough sleep, exercise, and eat and drink in a way that supports you to live your best life in and outside of the workplace.

8.   DO the activities in the book. It's important for you to write down or type out your answers, create the materials that are necessary to share with your network, and complete the practical activities to see results. If writing in the book doesn't work for you, start an *Awaken Your CAREERpreneur* journal or download a SUCCESSwork log from http://www.AwakenYourCareerpreneur.com.

9.   Set aside ample time each week to work through your SUCCESSwork. It can often take some time and experimentation to get to your best answer. Think of our time together not simply as the moments you sit down with the book but rather as the over 10,000 minutes in a week.

10.   Have fun! We do our best learning when me make our acquisition of knowledge enjoyable.

Part I

LAYING THE FOUNDATION

Chapter One

Creating the Vision

In a Twitter poll I administered about a year ago, I asked my followers to select what they believed to be the paramount skill successful people possess. About 30% picked effective interpersonal communication, another 20% picked a compelling vision, and the remaining 50% were scattered between skills in public speaking, embracing change, negotiation, and holding others accountable. None of this is very surprising because typically all of these skills are identified as fundamental to success. I was struck, however, that a number of responders wrote to me and asked why authenticity was not on my list.

I have to admit that I felt like I had egg on my face. While I have long asserted that authenticity is the foundation for success, a killer relationship, and anything and everything else that is good and fulfilling, I had never framed it as a skill. And it most certainly is! Living and working authentically is not an inborn ability. Rather, it is a lifelong process to strip away the layers of artifice we build up and make habitual over our lifetimes. In a culture that often rewards the newest, most clever and flashy idea, many of us make choices, forge relationships, and pursue courses of action that we think will make us the people we believe others want us to be. When we do this, we lose more and more of ourselves along the way. As a culture we have seen countless ideas, individuals, and organizations launch to success from innovative campaigns that by no means expressed the true identity of the person, product, or service.

So let us pause for a moment and remember what has happened to Enron, who had the seemingly customer-centered slogan *ask why*, and Countrywide, which claimed *demonstrate integrity, be a positive influence,* and *be an agent of change* were its top three values. Yup. We observe that flash and falsity might initially enable something or someone to take flight. However, flash and falsity will also, sooner rather than later, cause it to crash right down. The more that we as individuals are honest and genuine, the greater our ability to create a positive impact and build the foundation for lasting success.

A fellow business coach, Candye Hinton, describes the coaching principle of a personal foundation as *"the underpinning of your life. It is the platform from which you build your business and your relationships. Just as your house needs a strong foundation to support both its weight as well as to withstand the harsh elements of nature, so do humans."* In our SUCCESSwork during the first few chapters, we will ensure that you have the personal foundation necessary to sustain professional success throughout your career.

What's in a Vision?

> *"Somehow I can't believe that there are any heights that can't be scaled by a man who knows the secrets of making dreams come true. This special secret, it seems to me, can be summarized in four Cs. They are curiosity, confidence, courage, and constancy, and the greatest of all is confidence. When you believe in a thing, believe in it all the way, implicitly and unquestionably."* (Walt Disney)

A vision is a road map for *who* and *where* you want to be. It allows you to project forward and define the big picture. A compelling vision taps all of the senses—sight, smell, touch, taste, and sound. It enables you to describe and integrate the different facets in your life in a way that is meaningful and possible. Once you begin to articulate your vision, you can work backwards and design action steps (as you will in upcoming chapters) to close the gap from where you are to where you aspire to be.

One of the greatest visioning exercises I ever engaged in occurred after Winter Ball of my junior year in high school. I rarely had a date to a high school dance, and this Winter Ball was no exception. My friend Samantha had tried to shake me out of my malaise by setting me up with one of her friends. Unfortunately, at least for me, he went and broke his arm the day of the dance meaning I played third wheel to Samantha and her new boyfriend the entire night. When we made it back to her house after the dance, the two of us curled up on her couch and individually made a list of all of the qualities we sought in a future mate. Samantha, of course, essentially just described her new guy. Having had a lot of crushes, mostly on guys who couldn't have told you my name even if their lives depended on it, I decided to make a Top 100 List of qualities, life experiences, and opinions my future husband would have. Having never had a boyfriend, I had nothing to restrict my visioning.

I forgot about this list during my final year of high school, through my college years, and during a tumultuous relationship with my first boyfriend. It was a very pleasant surprise to discover it when I sorted through adolescent memorabilia prior to moving in with my second boyfriend, who ultimately became my husband. And wouldn't you know it, from such specific criteria as playing a musical instrument and having lived in another country to more general and yet no less important qualities like never raising his voice and taking time to come to an important decision, Steve met 98 of my 100 Must Haves. (In case you're wondering, the two he didn't make are being taller than me, probably one of the least important criteria a person could have for her life partner, and not having a piercing. Unbeknownst to me at sixteen, my future mate's nipple ring would turn out to be one of my favorite aesthetic qualities about him, just behind his always perfectly bronzed skin and crooked dimples!).

Back on Samantha's couch, had I restricted myself to my actual experiences with boys, I would have struggled to articulate criteria beyond "knows my last name" and "doesn't spit on himself when he talks." Fortunately for me, and my future offspring, I aimed a little bit higher. In the midst of a night of horrible insecurity and disappointment, I dared to define the partner I yearned to spend my life with and set the ball in motion for recognizing this man when he showed up in my life earlier than I could have possibly imagined.

Equally important to this process was letting go of the list. This is a place where a lot of aspiring CAREERpreneurs can get stuck. While we want to be clear on what we desire for ourselves, it's important for us to be open to the myriad ways these yearnings can show up in our lives. When we get too locked into specifics, whether it be, "my future mate must be a Jewish attorney on track for partner at a top New York City law firm" or "I need to be the Executive Director of a nonprofit arts agency by my fortieth birthday," we actually get in our own way of success because we are trying too hard to manipulate a particular outcome. CAREERpreneurs understand that sustainable success hinges on as much *being* as *doing*.

As you move through *your* SUCCESSwork in the coming pages, you may feel like your answers are incomplete or that the fulfillment of your vision is very far off. I get it. I've been there. Remember that your musings, like life, are a work-in-progress. Believe that you can engineer the life you desire, and start by finding the courage, focus, and commitment to write something down for each question I ask. If you hit upon a question asking you to consider an area that is not in your life and never will be, then and only then should you leave it blank.

SUCCESSwork: The Life Spheres

Directions: For each of the Life Sphere categories listed below, answer the following 2 questions as clearly as possible:

1.   What does it mean for you be *STRONG in this area?
2.   How *STRONG are you in this area currently?

*By strong, I am referring to the ability both to feel fulfilled and also to have a reserve should you experience any anticipated or unforeseen obstacles. For example, one of my coaching clients has said that for her, being strong in HEALTH/EXERCISE means staying 5 to 8 pounds under her target weight. This way she can eat dessert occasionally, enjoy a dinner party or a holiday, and continue to feel good about her body.

CAREER | The Life Spheres

1. What does it mean for you be STRONG in this area?

2. How STRONG are you in this area currently?

HOME

1. What does it mean for you be STRONG in this area?

2. How STRONG are you in this area currently?

FAMILY   The Life Spheres

1. What does it mean for you be STRONG in this area?

2. How STRONG are you in this area currently?

LEISURE/RECREATION

1. What does it mean for you be STRONG in this area?

2. How STRONG are you in this area currently?

SPIRITUALITY   The Life Spheres

1. What does it mean for you be STRONG in this area?

2. How STRONG are you in this area currently?

HEALTH/EXERCISE

1. What does it mean for you be STRONG in this area?

2. How STRONG are you in this area currently?

ROMANCE The Life Spheres

1. What does it mean for you be STRONG in this area?

2. How STRONG are you in this area currently?

FRIENDSHIPS

1. What does it mean for you be STRONG in this area?

2. How STRONG are you in this area currently?

FINANCE   The Life Spheres

1. What does it mean for you be STRONG in this area?

2. How STRONG are you in this area currently?

SELF-GROWTH

1. What does it mean for you be STRONG in this area?

2. How STRONG are you in this area currently?

Questions for Reflection

From the answers you have come up with thus far, what are the two areas of life where you feel the strongest?

How can you continue to keep these areas strong?

Which are the two areas that most need some buffing up?

What will you commit to undertaking in order to strengthen these areas?

What will be the payoff for the work you are undertaking?

SUCCESSwork: The Vision Board

Directions: Create a vision board that represents where you would like to be in each of the spheres of your life.

Physicists, psychologists, and coaches agree that when you put your attention to what you are hoping to achieve and give physical and visual representation to it, you move yourself creatively and efficiently towards goal achievement. (I'd be remiss if I didn't mention that I put *The Wall Street Journal* logo on my vision board a week before a writer from the publication, who I did not know, called for an interview!)

Like the previous SUCCESSwork, your vision board will likely be a work-in-progress. Aim to fill at least half of it and then continue to add, rearrange, and transition out items so that your board is constantly articulating where you are striving to go (and how you plan to embark on that journey) next. Ideally, your vision board should be adjusted every few months, before a big goal is undertaken, or after one has been achieved.

Your vision board can incorporate words, quotes, mementos, logos, images, photographs, and other pictures that reflect who and where you want to be as you move through your career. Remember to address all of the spheres of life, select items that engage all of your senses, and be open to the myriad possibilities for how your vision can take shape.

Note that there is no right way to create a vision board. There is only *your* best way. Make sure that your board speaks to your personality and inspires you to realize your dreams. Place it somewhere you will look at it often (e.g., next to your desk or opposite your bed).

SUCCESSwork: You Got Hired!

Now that you've done some overall life visioning, it's time to explore what your next professional step will look like. Regardless of whether you are in your dream job, itching to move into a new industry, or perhaps are seeking to create a new business or stream of revenue for an existing one, dare to identify what you are moving towards.

Directions: Write a letter to yourself from a company or client offering you your next opportunity.

This offer should be possible given your education, experiences, and the context (e.g., field, geographical location, etc.) even if it feels like it's a stretch. (Remember: CAREERpreneurship is a lifelong journey where you constantly strive towards new levels of possibility. Don't underestimate yourself, and don't be afraid to aim high!) **In this letter, which should be addressed from a person from a company that you would like to work for or have as a client, you want to identify as clearly as possible:**

1. A name and description for the opportunity
2. Salary or fee (and benefits, if applying for a job)
3. Key responsibilities, accountabilities, and tasks
4. What a typical day in the job will look like (if applying for a position)
5. Why the company/client picked you out of 100 other contenders

You may be asking, "Alexia, why am I aiming to make the letter as detailed as possible when you keep telling me to be open to the range of ways success can unfold for me?" I promise that I'm not trying to be difficult. Or confusing. Rather, I want you to buff up a variety of complementary muscles that are core to CAREERpreneurship—the ones necessary to honor success as your birthright as well as the ones that let you receive what the universe has in store for you. So stick with our dance between the micro and the macro vision.

When you have finished with your letter, go ahead and place it on your vision board. It's now time for one last bit of introspection to tie up this first chapter on personal foundation.

Questions for Reflection

What have you learned about the type of position/opportunity you are striving for?

What experiences, strengths, values, or other traits enabled you to stand out?

What is one thing you can do this week to move yourself closer to receiving your desired offer?

Now, congratulations are in order. You have identified what strength looks like in each life sphere, created a vision board, and identified the type of career opportunity you are working towards (while staying open for other juicy possibilities that might be coming on down your way). Most importantly, you have proven to yourself that your success and happiness cannot be put on hold, and you have taken a variety of steps to activate them. (Remember: if you need some support translating your SUCCESSwork into action, download a Weekly Log from http://www.AwakenYourCareerpreneur.com).

Chapter Two

Eliminating Barriers

I hope you have had a great time so far exploring where you are in the different spheres of life as well as who you want to be and what you seek to achieve through your career. This is necessary work for building a solid personal foundation from which you can take action, meet your goals, and sustain your success.

In Chapter 2 we will look at an equally important, corresponding part of the success process—getting rid of individual ways of being that undermine our ability to achieve our greatest potential.

> *"Our deepest fear is not that we are inadequate. Our deepest fear is that we are powerful beyond measure. It is our Light, not our Darkness, that most frightens us."* (Marianne Williamson)

If I were to ask you, (and I am going to), *"Identify 5 ways you sabotage your success,"* what would you say?

1. _____

2. _____

3. _____

4. _____

5. _____

I've asked this question to a lot of people over the years and the lack of diversity in answers will probably not surprise you. They typically include:

1. Second-guessing myself
2. Perfectionism
3. Overanalyzing options
4. Taking on more than I can handle
5. And perhaps the most commonly given answer, Procrastination!

Look over *your* answers for a moment. Now, ask yourself to pick one self-sabotaging habit that, if eliminated, would likely have the greatest impact on your success. Have you got it? Good. Now eliminate it!

Positive psychologist Dr. Sonja Lyubomirsky has identified that it takes approximately 11 weeks to solidify a new habit. Whether it's reprogramming one's self to exercise or taking accountability for one's choices, Lyubomirsky explains in her book, *The How of Happiness: A New Approach to Getting the Life You Want,* that it takes just 11 weeks of intentional, daily work to shift to the new way of being. At first, we may find ourselves having a hard time adapting our behavior. If we stick it out, though, and push through that uncomfortable period. If we really believe we can leave our old way of being behind, we really can reprogram ourselves. And there's no day like the present one to begin.

SUCCESSwork: Go from Symptom to Source

Directions: Bring to mind an unproductive habit you are going to eliminate. Now, before you set out to stop doing it, which although it is a praiseworthy aim rarely works, take some time to complete this next assignment to understand what is underneath it.

How many smokers do you know who quit smoking cold turkey and never touched another cigarette? (To be fair, my husband recently did hit his twelfth smoke-free anniversary. However, of the dozens of smokers I have known and worked with, he is the only one who achieved success this way). So having an *aha moment* and subsequently taking big, bold action can change your life. Most of us experience a succession of *aha's*, however, and it's the process of going from symptom to source that really facilitates our success. Now, think about the various points over the last week when you gave in to your nasty habit.

What was going on for you just before you did *it*?

_____

_____

_____

Who were you with?

_____

_____

_____

Where were you?

_____

_____

_____

What time of day was it?

_____

_____

_____

What emotion(s) were you feeling?

_____

_____

_____

What thoughts were going through you head?

_____

_____

_____

Next, consider what happened for you after you performed the behavior.

What was going on for you within the first few minutes?

_____

_____

_____

An hour later?

_____

_____

_____

A day after?

_____

_____

_____

Whether our habit is _saying no_ to opportunities because we doubt our abilities or overeating to obtain control when we feel out of balance, we might feel better for a short time after we give in to the habit. Typically, we then go right back to how we felt before we took action. That is because our habit is a symptom of something going on with us at a much deeper level.

Questions for Reflection

As you read through your answers to the above questions, what have you discovered might be the root cause(s) of your unproductive habit?

Over the next week, how can you both take intentional daily action to stop the habit and address its source?

How would you name or describe the new, useful habit you will replace the old one with?

And finally, how can you employ source vs. symptom thinking in other facets of your professional and personal life to come up with solutions that work for the various challenges you are experiencing?

Now, I need to be honest with you. This is going to be some of the toughest SUCCESSwork you tackle. However, the payoff will also be some of the largest! And I know. I never ask anyone I partner with to do something I haven't been willing to do myself.

You see, when I was growing up through the better part of my twenties, I had this belief that if I thought too much about something I wanted or told anyone about it that I was ensuring I would not get it. So I spent the better part of my childhood, adolescence, and early-career hiding my aspirations from others. While this may not have had a huge impact on me as a little one, it certainly did as I got older. I lost parts in ballets and plays, missed out on promotions, and undoubtedly did a lot of damage energetically. It wasn't enough for me to wake up one day and say, *"I'm going to start telling people what I want and then it's going to happen."* For I did do this, at least half a dozen times, and each time the thing I declared I wanted didn't go my way, I just fell more deeply into my self-sabotaging thinking. In order to let go of this habit, I had to get to the source. Fear. I needed to identify the messages I was telling myself as I narrated my day. *"You already missed your big opportunity." "You're pretty decent at a lot of things but not an expert at any of them."* And my favorite, *"You're the only person from your childhood who isn't famous. What did you do wrong?"* (For a long time I swore that if you were a talent agent in search of the next bright star in television, film, sports, or even marine biology, you should pull out one of my elementary school yearbooks to find your meal ticket). I spent a little too much time in college and graduate school playing Six Degrees of Alexia Vernon.

And yet rather magically, when I got serious about naming this mental crud I was carrying around with me, I jumpstarted some rather nice shifts. I realized that passing on opportunities to dance professionally or to pursue sketch comedy were blessings rather than curses. While I loved opening *New York Magazine* or *Vogue* and seeing interviews with old friends, I really wouldn't have wanted to have spent my life pursuing a singular focus like ballet or improv.

And wouldn't you know it, once I replaced the fear that I wasn't enough with some laughter at my misdirected insecurity, I started to see my own platform build and star rise. Suddenly, I had advocates in my professional and personal life helping me to get my needs and desires met. And opportunities I did not even know I wanted started showing up.

SUCCESSwork: Busting Tolerations

Some situations, ideas, kinds of work, environments, and even people just do not work for us. They make us feel cranky, bored, uncomfortable, and as a result, take us away from the possibility-centered mindset that is vital for achieving and sustaining goals. So let's get to some busting!

Directions: Identify and make a list of the Top 50 Things You *Tolerate.

(A *<u>toleration</u> is a re-occurring nuisance that we put up with, although it soaks up our time, energy, and enthusiasm). When we make the choice to tolerate something that undermines our success, we give away our personal power. We make excuses for not fulfilling our potential, perpetuate the habit of underperforming, and prevent ourselves from living satisfying professional and personal lives.

Tolerations can be environmental. *I don't have enough light in my office. I need more file space to stay organized.* Tolerations might also be related to people and relationships in our lives. *My father and I haven't spoken in ten years, yet I think about him all of the time, particularly around holidays. My ex and I still hang out and it drives my new partner crazy.* In addition, tolerations can be self-imposed in the form of our beliefs. So now, be honest with yourself, and identify those top fifty tolerations.

My Top 50 Tolerations

1. _____

2. _____

3. _____

4. _____

5. _____

6. _____

7. _____

8. _____

9. _____

10. _____

11. _____

12. _____

13. _____

14. _____

15. _____

16. _____

17. _____

18. _____

19. _____

20. _____

21. _____

22. _____

23. _____

24. _____

25. _____

26. _____

27. _____

28. _____

29. _____

30. _____

31. _____

32. _____

33. _____

34. _____

35. _____

36. _____

37. _____

38. _____

39. _____

40. _____

41. _____

42. _____

43. _____

44. _____

45. _____

46. _____

47. _____

48. _____

49. _____

50. _____

Questions for Reflection

What do you discover when listing your tolerations?

Do any themes emerge?

Who could you be, and what could you be doing with your time, if you were able to zap your tolerations for good?

Now, identify five tolerations that you will begin to fix over the next week. Make a plan for how you will continue to address your other tolerations as you move through the rest of the book.

My Top 5 Tolerations to Bust

1. Toleration: _____

Plan:

2. Toleration: _____

Plan:

3. Toleration: _____

Plan:

4. Toleration: _____

Plan:

> (blank box)

5. Toleration: _____

Plan:

> (blank box)

And remember, sometimes the easiest way to fix a toleration is to change your interpretation of the *thing* itself. For example, might the toleration be an opportunity to practice making the present perfect? Or an opportunity to forgive someone (possibly yourself) for the past? Or maybe even an opportunity simply to laugh at yourself or a situation?

David Romanelli, the author of *Yeah Dave's Guide to Livin' the Moment* says, "*As much as it's usually a reaction, laughter can also be a choice to treat rocky moments with joy the way you'd treat bland food with salt.*" Laughter is one of the best success-inducing habits to forge. It not only makes us feel better whenever we do it. It also injects a sense of play into the way we talk to ourselves and form our interpretations throughout our day.

SUCCESSwork: Recycle-the-Box

As I described above, sometimes the most powerful tolerations we cling to come in the form of limiting beliefs. These can have tremendous weight over how we see ourselves and as a consequence, impact how we show up to our lives and the way we see, record, and relive our experiences.

Directions: Think for a moment about what that voice in your head has said today.

Did the words you heard set you up to be successful? On a scale of 1-10, 1 representing having rhino rockets shoved up your nose to stop a nasal hemorrhage (I again speak from experience!) **and 10 representing eating a Mastro's Steakhouse chocolate soufflé** (It's worth a trip to a city with one!), **how much pleasure is that voice in your head bringing you?** Our gal Dr. Lyubomirsky, who we visited with earlier, says that 40% of our happiness is of our own choosing, while the remaining 60% is dictated by genetics and circumstance. This means almost half of our experience of life is up to us. This is great news whether you are currently dining on soufflé or having thick cotton objects stuck up your nostrils. For with practice, you can make experiencing life as a soufflé your new norm.

Now, make a list of the Top 10 beliefs that are not serving you well. Be honest with yourself here. I'm not asking you to analyze whether you are *entitled* to your belief or if it's *true*. I'm asking you to jot down any thinking that is holding you back from your full potential for success and life satisfaction.

1. _____

2. _____

3. _____

4. _____

5. _____

6. _____

7. _____

8. _____

9. _____

10. _____

Now, this is where the recycling comes in. **You are going to take each of your 10 beliefs and re-write them so that rather than presenting or reflecting a challenge or obstacle they shift you into seeing an opportunity.** Some examples from clients and other CAREERpreneurs who have dared to Recycle-the-Box include:

Initial Statement: *I don't have enough time to work on* _____ .
New Statement: *I have an opportunity to stop doing trivial tasks and putting others' needs before my own.*

Initial Statement: *I won't ever get over what* _____ *did.*
New Statement: _____ *has given me the greatest lesson of my life;* _____ *has taught me how to release the past, forgive, and as a result, heal.*

Initial Statement: *If I'm not <u>doing</u> something at all times, I'll never be able to get where I'm trying to go.*
New Statement: *We're called human <u>beings</u> for a reason. Remember to let go and breathe!*

What are *your* rewritten statements?

1. _____

2. _____

3. _____

4. _____

5. _____

6. _____

7. _____

8. _____

9. _____

10. _____

Some of your new statements, or mantras, are going to be more relevant and useful than others. **I want you to take the two or three New Statements that you most need to be reminded of, write them on some note cards, and post them in spots you find yourself when you often succumb to the Initial Statement.** Your New Statement really can become habitual. Again, just dare to embark on Day 1. We both know you have got it in you.

Questions for Reflection
How will you know when you have been able to Recycle-the-Box once and for all?

How might recycling some of your beliefs start a chain reaction of positive results in your CAREERpreneurship journey?

I want to acknowledge you for adding so many new ingredients to your recipe for career success—getting to the source of unproductive habits and replacing them with new ones, identifying and zapping your tolerations, and shifting limiting beliefs to empowering ones. Stay with it, especially when you find yourself questioning whether you really can cook up what you desire for yourself. I promise that the payoff is delicious!

Chapter Three

Unleashing My Potential

How does it feel to know that you are on your way to replacing self-defeating habits with empowering ones? How have you been doing getting to the *source* of ideas, concerns, and ways of being? How many limiting beliefs have you been able to *recycle*?

Now that you have both created the vision for success and learned how to get out of your own way so that you can best achieve it, in this chapter we are going to explore the cornerstone of showing up to each day of life as a CAREERpreneur.

CAREERpreneurs are leader in our careers, companies, and communities. To activate success, we harness our values, strengths, resources, and enthusiasms to empower others towards solutions that are good for the economy, society, and the environment. We might think of leaders as captains of industry, elected officials, and other people who oversee millions of people. However, leadership is a way of being and approaching action. Leadership is not a noun—a role or title we are given—it is a verb! It means that we are consistently engaged in purposeful work that creates and sustains the kinds of results we can be proud of. Effective leadership begins on an individual level. When we are clear on our values, strengths, resources, and enthusiasms, we can be self-directed in our lives and in our careers. We can empower ourselves, and as a result, those we collaborate with.

I have been blessed with a lot of models of effective CAREERpreneurship in my life, many of whom are in my own family. As a little one, my Aunt Elaine was the cat's pajamas to me. She left her small town of Pittsfield, Massachusetts at sixteen to dance with the New York City Ballet, by her early twenties was traveling the world as a model, and in her thirties had found her soul mate and appeared to have effortlessly built a career acting in theatre, television, and film. She and my Uncle Herb, a successful writer and producer, lived in the world's most adorable bungalow in the Hollywood Hills, and I yearned for any opportunity to hang out with them and their stylish industry friends. Reminiscing about sleepovers where I'd watch the sunrise through the shoji screen from my platform bed on the tatami mat in their authentic Japanese meditation room—the scent of incense from my Uncle Herb's office next door still wafting from the night before, fills me with an unparalleled sense of joy. Yet for all the sexiness in the way I've archived these sweet girlhood memories, the greatest lessons I have learned from my aunt are how to stay on the path of honoring one's purpose and adapting to unforeseen setbacks.

At a time when many performers and creative personalities simply fade from public view, my aunt made the choice to turn a longtime individual practice she shared with my Uncle Herb into the next chapter of her career trajectory. A student and advocate of the ancient energy healing practice of Feng Shui, my aunt and uncle decided to train with Grand Master Professor Thomas Lin Yu so that they could take their burgeoning passion to heal people's homes and businesses and build it into a business. While my aunt's story might easily have stopped with some testimonials of how she, along with my Uncle Herb, rather quickly built a thriving business (The Wright Way of Feng Shui) that enabled some of Hollywood's biggest personalities to reach new levels of peace and prosperity, it actually took a dramatic detour. When my Aunt Elaine lost my Uncle Herb, her best friend and business partner to cancer, she could have easily made the choice to hang up her shingle and surrender to her deserved grief. However, by this point I'm sure you can see where this narrative is going, and it ain't going there. My aunt instead said, "I've got more to give," and decided that the best way to honor my Uncle Herb's memory was to blaze forward, professionally and personally, and honor his legacy and her healing gifts by growing the business further, developing her own line of handmade crystals and jewelry, giving back to her community through serving on several women's entrepreneurial boards and at a local women's shelter, and most importantly, shifting this and the universe's subsequent curveballs into opportunities to learn, grow, and be of service.

As I've learned from watching my Aunt Elaine, in order to move CAREERpreneurship from a concept to a practice, we must not only understand what we are called to do (and recognize when that call changes), we must also understand how our gifts align with what's most needed (and will be paid for) by those we are seeking to impact. My aunt has had a keen understanding of who her clients are and has developed her offerings in a way that she can give people what they want so that she can give them what they need. CAREERpreneurship also requires that we have the ability to receive professional and personal challenges as lessons to toughen us up. So let's get to work on activating the next chapter of your own CAREERpreneurship journey.

What Are Your Core Values?

"Values are like fingerprints. Nobody's are the same, but you leave 'em all over everything you do." (Elvis Presley)

The cornerstone of CAREERpreneurship is to know your core values and take action from them. This is a hard one for a lot of us. We do not always see our so-called leaders operating from such a place. From Hank Greenberg to Bernie Madoff to Tony Hayward, over the last decade many of our most prominent leaders have been the poster children for greed and a rampant misuse of power.

A core value is an enduring force in our life that excites us, makes us feel strong, and shapes our thoughts, feelings, and behaviors. Core values are freely chosen and representative of our deepest motivators. They remain relatively consistent throughout our lives. A true core value is not a need, an attachment, or something we believe we *should* care about. Rather, values motivate us to show up to all facets of our lives authentically and as our best selves. As a consequence, when we honor them, we make a greater contribution in what we do and with whom we engage.

SUCCESSwork: Core Values Checklist

Directions: Please identify your core values using the steps below.

Step One: Cross off the 10 values that are LEAST important to you. This will guard against selecting values you think you *should* pick and enable you to pick values that genuinely motivate you.

Step Two: Out of the remaining 10 values, pick the 3 that are MOST important to your life and highlight them for yourself. These 3 values represent your core values. They should be honored at all times for you to feel like you are fulfilling your purpose and operating from a place of *integrity*. To be living from such a place, one must act consistently in adherence to her values.

Values List

A)   **Achievement:** Accomplishing my goals

B)   **Innovation:** Creating new methods, practices, and ways of being

C)   **Adventure:** Exploring and risk taking

D)   **Personal Freedom:** Working independently and autonomously

E)   **Authenticity:** Showing up to life genuinely as myself

F)   **Excellence:** Pursuing the highest quality

G)   **Contribution:** Empowering others to achieve their full potential

H)   **Spirituality:** Connecting to a higher power and/or engaging in ongoing self-development

I)   **Power:** Influencing others

J)   **Responsibility:** Owning and being held accountable for my actions

K)   **Learning:** Committing to personal growth and pursuing knowledge

L)   **Meaningful Work:** Performing purposeful work that makes an impact

M)   **Respect:** Showing regard for others

N)   **Family:** Creating a happy and congenial living situation with people of my choosing

O) **Wisdom:** Possessing understanding and insight
P) **Justice:** Treating all living beings fairly and equitably
Q) **Recognition:** Ensuring that I am well-known and am thought of with prestige
R) **Security:** Sustaining a stable future
S) **Tradition:** Honoring and celebrating history and past practice
T) **Courage:** Attacking any real or self-imposed limitation

Questions for Reflection

On a scale of 1-10, 1 meaning never and 10 meaning always, how often are you currently making choices in thoughts, feelings, attitudes, and actions based on your core values?

What would a 10 look like for you?

What would need to happen to close the gap between where you are now and where you would like to be?

What kinds of careers, organizations, and business relationships would best enable you to honor your core values consistently?

When we know our core values, we can more quickly and effortlessly respond to the opportunities we are consciously crafting as well as those that we'd rather not have to deal with and show up anyway. Less than a year into building Catalyst for Action, my mom and stepdad in Las Vegas experienced a series of interlocking setbacks that sounded an alarm, or more accurately an intuitive voice, that said, *"Alexia, come home."* Family is one of my core values and while telling that voice, *"I can't move home right now, I've got too much taking off in New York,"* really was the seemingly logical thing to do, the times I attempted to find solutions to support my family where I did not relocate my new marriage and business to Las Vegas, I knew I was out of integrity. So after taking the better part of a year to chart how to viably head west, my husband and I did.

And aside from Day 4 of our cross-country trip to Las Vegas where Steve, still swollen from a fire ant attack on Day 2, hit a bat on the road and proceeded minutes later to take out the better part of the motel carport we thought we might crash at for the night (all of this, I might mention, happening in the wee hours of our one-year anniversary), I have never questioned my choice to relocate back west! That's what clarity on core values allows a CAREERpreneur, the confidence to know that when you make a choice based on keeping what's most important to you at the forefront, you really can do no wrong.

Playing to Strengths

If your core values motivate who you are through the actions you take in thinking, feeling, and behaving, your strengths are the means for ensuring you show up each day as this person and deliver on your professional purpose and promise. We can easily fall into a pattern of making choices to craft ourselves into the people we think others want us to be. This is detrimental for linking our calling to our career. For when we start to people please, we not only often fail to give other people what they in fact do want; we also typically lose more and more of ourselves along the way.

One HR Manager at a New York City fashion company shares, *"I like to take a close look at what prospective new hires are wearing to an interview because I want to see how they are conforming to trends. I'm looking for the people who are brave enough not to!"*

Although we have a tendency to focus on where we can do better rather than on those areas where we feel like superstars, leadership experts like Tom Rath, Barry Conchie, and Marcus Buckingham argue that we have the most impact, achieve our greatest results, inspire more people, and derive the greatest life satisfaction when we focus on our strengths. They have concluded that successful leaders across industries play to their strengths a minimum of 60-70% of the time in their work.

SUCCESSwork: Identify and Play to *Your* Strengths

Directions: Think through a typical week for yourself. Make a list of 10-20 tasks you typically engage in. The more specific you can be the better.

Examples could include:

- Cold calling prospective clients and presenting my 30-second pitch
- Creating departmental expense reports
- Searching online articles, editorials, and blogs for market research
- Facilitating New Hire training for groups of employees

My 10-20 Weekly Tasks

1. _____

2. _____

3. _____

4. _____

5. _____

6. _____

7. _____

8. _____

9. _____

10. _____

11. _____

12. _____

13. _____

14. _____

15. _____

16. _____

17. _____

18. _____

19. _____

20. _____

From each of the 2 categories below, you are going to go back to this list and put 1 letter next to each of your tasks.

Category 1- Sense of Enjoyment

   If you enjoy this activity, you are going to put down- "E"

   If this activity brings you displeasure, you are going to put down- "D"

   If you are neutral about this activity, you are going to put down- "N"

Category 2- Sense of Skill

   If you feel skilled in this activity, you are going to put down- "S"

   If you feel unskilled in this activity, you are going to put down- "U"

   If you feel just adequate about your skill, you are going to put down- "A"

Now, you are going to review your list and look for activities where you have both an "E" and an "S." These are your strengths. You are good at these activities AND find them pleasurable. **Also, make sure to note for yourself where you have a "D" and a "U."** These are activities you want to avoid like the H1N1 flu virus!

If you find that you have either too many strengths or not enough of them, consider being more specific with context. To pull from our examples, it may be that you wrote down that you don't enjoy "Facilitating New Hire trainings for groups of employees." Perhaps this is true when the groups are over twenty people. However, when you have the opportunity to train five to ten people, you get to speak *with* rather than *at* your audience, coach more, talk less, and in this arrangement you come alive.

On the flipside, you may discover that "Facilitating New Hire Training for groups of employees" is a strength *except* when you have to train first-time employees. Perhaps this group wants more of a technology-based learning environment, and you prefer to deliver something hands-on and experientially. Try asking the following contextual questions: *How many people make this the case? In what kind of environments does this ring true?* These will help you discover the sources of strengths and how to design and attract opportunities for leveraging them. After all, what person wants to be delivering New Hire Training if passionate about Diversity?

It was through asking myself the kinds of questions I have asked you to consider that I realized that I had to leave the last full-time job I held prior to launching Catalyst for Action. Although I could have placed an "S" by 90% of my reoccurring tasks and responsibilities, I also could have placed a "D" by over 60% of them. When my small department got slashed and I wound up wearing both manager and administrator hats, I suddenly found myself creating one expense report after another. Even worse, I lived in front of the copy machine and file cabinet, creating and organizing materials for colleagues and clients. And I hate cleaning the way most people hate snakes. Or the IRS. Or fingernails on a chalkboard. (So I'm sure you won't be surprised to learn that "a love of vacuuming" is on my Top 100 partner qualities list!)

Knowing the activities we are good at AND enjoy ensures that we are making the best possible contribution to the world and embarking on sustainable work. It also creates the conditions necessary for *flow*, what author and creativity expert Mihály

Csíkszentmihályi says is what *"makes a life worth living."* For when we are able to consistently perform our work in *"a state in which [we] are so involved in an activity that nothing else seems to matter,"* Csíkszentmihályi's definition of *flow*, we know we are playing to our strengths.

Now, let's get back to *your* discoveries about *your* strengths.

Questions for Reflection

What have you discovered about you strengths?

How often have you been playing to them in your most recent role(s)?

What would a new role need to look like for you to engage your strengths on a regular basis and experience a state of *flow*?

What small changes could you make in your professional and personal life to play to these strengths more regularly, starting TODAY?

SUCCESSwork: Bring Out the Jazz Hands

Although I cannot carry a tune, I've always had a fondness for musicals. I find the idea of people having so much emotion and passion that they must break out into song and dance incredibly appealing. Whenever I'm about to speak before a group, I amp myself up by singing along to Lea Michele's version of *Don't Rain On My Parade*. It not only gives me an opportunity to warm up my vocal chords, it also lets me cry—just a little—loosen up, get in touch with my emotions, and ensure I connect to my audience once I get into the room.

> *What would it take for you to show up to each day of your life with jazz hands?*

In your last SUCCESSwork, you had an opportunity to identify tasks that you are good at and enjoy. Often times, however, we have interests and concerns we have never had an opportunity to account for or indulge. While I hope you approach all of your SUCCESSwork with a healthy balance of focus and playfulness, for this one I am going to ask you to go put yourself in a space that really resonates with your spirit and makes you feel fully alive. Truly, get up and move outside to your garden or draw a warm bath. Get that tushie moving. Bring with you any accoutrement that will help enliven the experience. I suggest candles, lavender essential oil, dark chocolate, and if you have more traditionally masculine sensibilities, consider a musk scent or even a beer.

Directions: Now that you are in your spot, give yourself a few minutes to take it all in. Tap into all of your senses and digest the environment you have created. Put everything it took to get you to this spot and everything you have to do once you leave on hold. Take some nice, full-bodied breaths. With each, slow your breathing down a little bit more. Enjoy being in your body and living fully in the present moment. Once you have given yourself ample opportunity to unwind, move through the following 10 questions at a pace that feels right for you.

1. If you were to describe your *purpose* in the world in one sentence, how would you do it?

     _____

     _____

     _____

     _____

     _____

     _____

2. What is the greatest compliment you have received? If you could receive another great compliment, what would it be? Who would say it? What would make it significant?

     _____

     _____

     _____

     _____

     _____

3. If you could combat one social problem in the world, what would it be? And how would being a part of the solution impact your sense of self?

     _____

     _____

     _____

     _____

4. What is a topic you have always wanted to learn more about? What about it piques your interest?

_____

_____

_____

_____

_____

_____

5. What city in the world best represents who you are *right now*? What city best represents who you are *becoming*?

_____

_____

_____

_____

_____

_____

6. If you had to repeat just one task for the rest of your working life, what would it be? Why?

_____

_____

_____

_____

_____

_____

7.   What three people have most inspired you in your life? How?

_____

_____

_____

_____

_____

_____

8.   What is the one lesson you have learned and never need to learn again?

_____

_____

_____

_____

_____

_____

9.   How will you know if you have lived a successful life? What do you want your legacy to be?

_____

_____

_____

_____

_____

_____

10. What is the question you were born to answer?

_____

_____

_____

_____

_____

Questions for Reflection

What connections can you draw between your answers and your values and strengths?

What opportunities for aligning these three areas (enthusiasms, values, and strengths) emerge?

If new enthusiasms popped up, how can you start honoring them and explore how to incorporate them into your career?

SUCCESSwork: I Am My Own Best Resource

Directions: Make a List of the Top 10 Success Resources that you possess.

In your final SUCCESSwork of the chapter, you are going to explore one last foundational element of CAREERpreneurship, *resources. Many of us have a tendency to think if only we had _____, then we would _____. CAREERpreneurs recognize the resources they already have access to and tap them before focusing on and trying to achieve what they lack.

A *<u>resource</u> is any *thing* that can help us achieve the results we desire. It could be **material** (e.g., Microsoft Publisher), **geographical** (e.g., living near a new company who needs people like me), **psychological** (e.g., a useful mantra or belief system), a **relationship** (e.g., the mother of a family friend is on the board of a company I'd like to work for), or a **service** (e.g., free photocopying on a college campus). The sky truly is the limit.

Don't worry about seeing how the resources you identify can catalyze the particular brand of success you seek. Save that for later reflection. For now, just focus on observing and tracking the resources you possess yet may have not thought about or capitalized on for a while.

My Top 10 Success Resources

1. _____

2. _____

3. _____

4. _____

5. _____

6. _____

7. _____

8. _____

9. _____

10. _____

Questions for Reflection

How can the resources you identified help you close the gap from where you are to where you want to be?

[ ]

What are the two resources you possess that can have the greatest impact on your success, and how will you make sure that you maximize them?

[ ]

How can you link the resources you have to the connections you have drawn between your values, strengths, and enthusiasms?

[ ]

If *effective leadership* is harnessing your values, strengths, resources, and enthusiasms to empower others towards solutions that are good for the economy, society, and environment, how would you describe yourself as a leader?

As you continue to chart your unique CAREERpreneurship path, check in frequently with your values, strengths, resources, and enthusiasms to ensure you are continuing to align them. Build time into your week, and ideally into each day, to disengage from technology and resist the need to multi-task. Nourish yourself by just *being*. See what lives in the space around you. Listen to the naturally occurring sounds. Touch the architecture. Smell the scents (the good, the bad, and the confusing). When you quiet the chatter in your head, you allow you heart to open and your gut, or intuition, to speak.

Chapter Four

Who Needs Me Most?

Although I'm not an economist, as a career expert I nevertheless believe it is important to situate who you are in the process of becoming within the realities of the marketplace. While the personal foundation work you have been engaging in is necessary for thriving in any economy, how you develop your career should be framed by where opportunities exist and will be growing.

In one of my favorite books, *A Whole New Mind*, Daniel Pink explains why, in "the future," those who are creative and empathic (e.g., teachers, inventors, and designers) will have the most coveted set of skills. He does a survey of the evolution of the American economy from Agricultural (18th -19th Century), to Industrial (19th - 20th Century), to Information (20th - 21st Century), to Conceptual (21st Century and Beyond). If the Agricultural Age was about the farmer, the Industrial Age about the factory worker, the Information Age about the knowledge worker, then I'm going to posit that the Conceptual Age is about a very particular type of creator. It calls for those who design solutions that are for the social, economic, and environmental sustainability of our planet.

I turn to my early life as a dancer for a lot of metaphors on success, creativity, innovation and CAREERpreneur0ship, for dance is all about pushing the self further than we imagine it can go. It's about using an expressive, gesture-based vocabulary to tell a story and move an audience to think and to feel. And dancers themselves are the quintessential CAREERpreneurs. Most move between dancing, teaching, choreographing, and typically have to use dance as a launching pad to a new professional chapter by the time they hit their thirties, an age where CAREERpreneurs in other fields are just beginning to hit their stride. See how these three dancers, who embody Pink's necessary minds for the Conceptual Age, have engineered their own road maps for professional success, creative fulfillment, and societal contribution.

A Tale of Three Dancers

Alexia: How would you describe what you currently do?

Amanda Brotman (President, Amanda Pearl): I run a small accessories company, playing many roles in the process—managing design, product development, sourcing, production, sales, marketing, corporate philanthropy, bookkeeping, and acting as the "cleaning staff." Much of the day is spent attending to urgent issues and requests and working on the operational aspects of the business. The rest is spent on discovering new materials, gathering inspiration, developing new products, and thinking up creative ways to get these products in front of the eyeballs and into the hands of potential buyers. I am also very interested in having my business not be just another contributor of "stuff" to the planet, but using it to highlight causes I think are important, so I also try to read and learn about organizations whose work I would like to support through my business.

Brittany Fridenstine-Keefe (Dancer and Educator): In addition to being a freelance dancer, I teach ballet, improvisation, and a specialized system of movement called GYROTONICÒ. I teach in Manhattan, both at a commercial studio and out of my home studio, as well as in dance schools around the country. Each of these "jobs" is based in my passion to move and help others move more efficiently and healthily.

Aubrey Lynch (Leadership Consultant and Certified Life Coach): There isn't one title that I wear that explains all that I do which I think is a good thing even in a world that likes clean and clear categories. Officially, I am a Leadership Consultant and Certified Life Coach, and I always wear those hats while doing everything else that I do. I am on faculty at The Ailey School and choreograph. I also lead workshops that I have designed and give keynotes on both arts and non-arts related topics. In addition, I am master of ceremonies when asked and I love it. I remain open to anything else that has to do with human connection and evolution.

Alexia: What about your work gets you the most jazzed?

Amanda: I love to build, develop and grow things. So to see something come to together after all of the blood, sweat and tears—there is really no greater pleasure. I always liken the business to a million-piece puzzle. It takes a lot of time to even *begin* to get the pieces in place, but after a while, one can begin to see the image take shape. One has to be patient and diligent and keep working to get things in order, bit by bit. Whether it is seeing a design come to life, seeing someone on the street with an Amanda Pearl, or seeing one of my designs in a publication, there's really nothing more satisfying and it motivates me and gets me *jazzed* to keep pushing forward.

Brittany: I gain a great degree of fulfillment pushing my body, or someone else's body, to its fullest potential. I find the personal connections I create with other people, as a catalyst to them achieving greater health and an understanding of what they are capable of, most rewarding.

Aubrey: The common thread in all that I do is human connection and awareness. I love the *aha* self-discovery moments. This can be as simple as a student learning something new about a transition in a dance class, or as profound as an audience full of people grasping a new way of looking at larger life issues. Being the conduit of leadership from the inside out and pointing people towards seeing and being their truth keeps me energized.

Alexia: In what ways did dance prepare you for this stage of your CAREERpreneurship journey?

Amanda: A dancer is not much different from an entrepreneur in any other business or industry. A dancer's body and her talent is her product. She must work at perfecting her product by practicing her technique and doing strength training in order to gain a competitive advantage in an industry with far more dancers than jobs. My new industry and career are no different. There are hundreds of accessory designers for every one designer that "makes it" and is successful in the category. Because of my background in dance, competition, focused drive, and the need to be exceptional at what I do are not alien concepts. This mindset is ingrained in me and will undoubtedly help me to be successful in my new career outside of the dance world.

Brittany: The process of becoming a dancer involves rigorous training and steely determination to overcome the many obstacles one encounters en route to building a career. This process also cultivates constant curiosity around how to better understand the body. These lessons all prepared me for the many paths of my current work. Through the challenges I encountered as a dancer, I also learned the reality of politics and how to remain determined—to strengthen my resolve— when obstacles appear. I am not where I dreamed I would be when I was young and first began my dance training. In fact, I am in a more interesting place than I ever envisioned. I am perhaps less famous that I childishly dreamed, but as a person and as an artist, the determination that I had to muster up created more balance in my life and also opened up interesting options that I could not have imagined for myself before.

Aubrey: Dance has played a very interesting role in where I am now. There are the obvious perks like discipline, endurance, and presentation, how to stand, what to wear, and how to enter a room. Dance experience also comes in really handy when using movement in workshops. However, I have discovered that the art of moving onstage has had an even more profound effect. When I was able to let go of the thinking that can often cloud a performance and trust my training, music, and preparation, I was completely free and connected with my purest and most authentic self. There was a connection with other dancers who shared the space. There was a connection that extended out into the audience and dare I say it, to the universe. That may sound lofty and a bit Kumbaya, but this connectedness serves me now whether I am one-on-one with a client or with a large group.

Alexia: What have you had to learn and discover on your own?

Amanda: I was used to working with such disciplined individuals that I did not realize that the rest of the world doesn't necessarily have the same work ethic that I do. That has been one of the greatest challenges and lessons I have had to learn. Because the world of dance is all about practice, preparation, with every step planned out,

I have also had to retrain myself and learn to act on my feet and roll with the punches—something I was not at all used to having to do. In the ballet world there is not much improv, but this has turned out to be one of the most needed skills to survive in my new career.

Brittany: Because I became a professional dancer right out of high school, I needed to "grow-up" at a young age. At 17, I was just committed to dancing and trying to live successfully away from home and master the necessary life skills to do so. As my career progressed, "just being a dancer" was not enough. I have had to teach myself how to be a small business owner and learn all of the financial, planning, marketing, and customer relation skills that go along with that. I have also learned that growing young minds (or older ones) is less about "right or wrong" answers and more about developing critical thinking skills. And ultimately, it's about having compassion for the person or people before us.

Aubrey: When I left Alvin Ailey American Dance Theater, I did not know what was next. I just knew that it was time to try other things. I had a sense that I would remain in the arts and that performance would be a big part of my future, but I was open to more. That was a scary time. I went from gig to gig never knowing where any of it was leading or if it was leading anywhere. I was just doing what I loved. When the money really got low and it seemed like everything was about to go south, along came a lion. *The Lion King* took me on an eleven-year journey filled with rich experiences that would have been impossible to know anything about before leaving Ailey. I'm there again now in mid leap, not completely sure where I will land. I'm just in the air juggling my many hats and loving each one that I wear. Experience has taught me that when I come down, I will land in a place that was unimaginable at the time of take off!

Alexia: What did the road trip between dancing to what you are currently doing look like?

Amanda: After dancing, I had to find a new path and a new passion. I had other interests, but I had no idea how those translated into a career and knew it was going to take lots of trial and error. The first step was to get my college education, so I moved to New York to study art history at Barnard College. I was also very interested in fashion design, so I signed up for Parsons' Summer Fashion Design intensive in Paris, and I took internships in fashion publishing and with a fashion design house. I ended up working for Marc Jacobs out of college where I got an on the job crash course in product development, raw materials sourcing and development, technical design, and production. All of the experiences from the time I left dance through my tenure at Marc Jacobs pushed me along the path and led me to develop the confidence, desire, and wherewithal to start my own business.

Brittany: I began teaching dance early in my career as a means to increase my income. I have always enjoyed teaching, but until recently it was more of a side job than something that I valued as much as my dancing. I think at a certain point in my career I began feeling that the life of a dancer is an inherently selfish pursuit. The hours in front of a mirror obsessing over my own movement and physique, the quest for an audience reaction and relationship, the approval of a director; all of these preoccupations are necessary but started to feel hollow. I began looking at the variety of skills that I had acquired and considered how I could use them to give back. The life of a dancer also includes an off-season and during one such time, with some financial assistance through Career Transitions for Dancers, I took my first GYROTONICÒ certification course.

Aubrey: I talk a lot about following what you love and leaping even if you are not sure how things will work out. I believe that if you put it out in the universe, the universe responds loud and clear. The first time I did this was when I left the University of Michigan. I was there on a chemistry scholarship and was only dancing for fun on the side. I wanted to give dancing a real try to see what would happen if I gave it my all. Coming from a small town, I had no idea that one could actually make a living dancing. I dropped my unfinished degree and moved to New York against my parents' wishes. Twenty-five summers later here I am in a career that no chemistry degree could have given me! Not that we should all drop our formal education and run off to join the circus. Being sensible while going after our passion can lead to an amazing life. The road from dance to where I am now has been just like that first leap, the leap that really set my career in motion. It has been a series of sensible risks towards the things I love. There has been lots of unknowing and many sleepless nights. However, time and time again, things have fallen into place by applying myself fully in the direction of my heart.

Alexia: If you could time travel 2-5 years down the line, what do you envision as the next chapter of your CAREERpreneurship journey?

Amanda: I am looking forward to having the bulk of the pieces of my business puzzle in place—so that I can then see and develop the bigger picture. To not have so many of the little things be such a time consuming challenge will also allow me to spend more time on the creative aspects of the business. Hopefully this will also allow for a more balanced personal life so that I won't feel like such a crazy person and can spend more time with my family and even start one of my own.

Brittany: If life thus far has taught me anything, it is that you can't really predict what will happen or where you will be in the next 5 years. I intend to still be dancing, potentially be starting a family, and I will have completed my undergraduate degree. I enjoy the current diversity of work that I have created for myself in New York. However, I hope that I will have established a little bit more of a home base (the subway is my typical lunch spot at this juncture, and I don't know if that is the most sanitary option!).

Aubrey: I would like to continue helping people find their truths and achieve their dreams. As the performer in me will need to be continually fed, I intend to find a way to make this community impact happen in a large public forum, possibly through publications, internet, TV, and film. If I can find a way to marry the performer in me with the desire to help others, I will be living the life that I want. It's also important for me to travel and have lots of friends in lots of places. Although money is amazing and I hope to have lots of it, money has never been the goal. I am claiming a life of meaning and purpose filled with love and fun. Though I am not sure how it will happen, I know that it will!

The Emergence of a Green Economy

"I believe that creating a green career track is choosing to walk the talk of life purpose and sustainable living principles. For me, it's the juice of life. Making conscious career and personal choices that support sustainability and social justice. Working for a better world for generations to come!" (Barbara Parks, Co-Author of *The Complete Idiot's Guide to Green Careers*, Career Coach and Founder of Green Career Tracks)

The *green economy* or *green-collar jobs* have gotten a lot of spin since 2009, much the way information technology jobs did in the late 1980s and early 1990s. I'm going to boil down what you need to know about our greening economy into two key principles—know what a green economy is and understand how to leverage it in your CAREERpreneurship journey.

1.   A green economy is one that is built and sustained through jobs that provide a living wage, build strong communities locally and throughout the world, and respect and restore the environment. Such positions are cropping up in corporations, nonprofits, small businesses, the government, think tanks, elementary and secondary schools, and universities across the country. They can be found in such seemingly disconnected fields as business and finance, construction, renewable energy, education, marketing, law, city planning, wildlife management, fashion design, and hospitality, among others.

2.   Regardless of whether your education, experience, and enthusiasm lies in environmental science or another "green" field, you want to be able to answer the following:

   A)   How will my field (and the specific role(s) I'm looking to perform in it) need to evolve in order to meet the needs created by a green economy? (Remember, it doesn't just take solar panel manufacturers and installers to make solar energy. It takes the people who design the products, market them, design websites for them, teach people about them, etc.)

B) How can I gain the experience, knowledge, and relationships I will need to thrive in a green economy *now* so that I can show current and prospective employers and clients that *who* I am and *what* I do embraces principles of sustainability?

Profile of a "Green" Career

While "green" might sound so 2008 and beyond, green careers have been in existence for centuries. Look at the trajectory for one lifelong green professional, Dana E. Dolsen.

Dana E. Dolsen, Utah Human Dimensions

Dana is a citizen of the New World, born in Canada and a resident of the U.S. since 1987. He obtained his BS in Outdoor Recreation from Acadia University, Wolfville, Nova Scotia (NS), Canada (1975). Thereafter, Dana worked for the NS Lands and Forests, the City of Calgary, Alberta (AB), Keyano Community College and the YMCA (both in Fort McMurray, AB). He acquired an MS degree in Forest Science, specializing in Recreation Planning and Management at the University of Alberta, graduating in 1986.

In Canada, Dana was an Interpretive Planner for the Meewasin Valley Authority in Saskatoon, Saskatchewan. He also worked at Alberta Forestry, Lands and Wildlife as an analyst of biological and sociological factors affecting the province's first catch-and-release trout management policy, and later authored management plans for three provincially designated Alberta Public Lands' Natural Areas.

In 1987, Dana began working for the University of Idaho's National Park Service Park Studies Unit. In 1991, Dana became Montana Fish, Wildlife & Park's first Human Dimensions Specialist. He created the Program Outcomes Assessment Project process and initiated its first cycle in supporting that agency's efforts to move toward a Comprehensive Management System through the development of three separate divisional strategic plans. He was the lead investigator in the conduct of the Social Assessment of the Wildlife Programmatic Environmental Impact Statement.

From 1998-2009, Dana served as the Utah Division of Wildlife Resources (DWR) Wildlife Planning Manager. He successfully coordinated the development of the Congressionally required, Utah Comprehensive Wildlife Conservation Strategy, approved in September 2005. He spearheaded revising the Utah DWR Strategic Plan: 2007-2011, and he coordinated/coached employee implementation teams as they put strategies into action.

In 2009, Dana's position was transformed into the Human Dimensions Coordinator, where he coordinates the Leadership Development Program, designs and leads social science investigations on conservation outreach-social marketing campaigns, agency branding and culture enhancement, and supervises agency evaluations to measure trends for strategic planning purposes and partnership development.

SUCCESSwork: Know What's Out There

While I'm not a fan of limiting one's job search to newspaper listings and online job search engines, for anywhere from 70%-95% of jobs come from networking, I find these tools immensely useful for showing what jobs already exist and are most popular. Although these sites might only give you just an inkling of the opportunities in the current marketplace, for the rest are never even advertised, they can help you answer a bunch of valuable questions.

Directions: Pick 3-5 traditional online and print job search sites to scan for current openings. (Even if you're a business owner or consultant, consider perusing these sites to get a lay of the land and ensure that what you do is as relevant as possible.)

I recommend the following:

1. http://www.Indeed.com or http://www.SimplyHired.com
2. http://www.USAJobs.gov/
3. http://Jobs.Change.org/

4.   http://www.Idealist.org

5.   http://www.Thingamajob.com/Browse-Jobs/

6.   Your city, county, and state Human Resources website

YES, most of these sites have a green jobs slant. That's intentional!

If something really juicy pops up, certainly, feel free to apply. Remember, however, the goal here is just to gather some information on emerging opportunities you may have not known about. You will keep compiling the strategies and techniques to dynamize your candidacy in the coming chapters.

You are aiming to learn the following:

1.   What kinds of positions are available in your field?

2.   What kinds of education and experience do they want?

3.   What skills are desired?

4.   What are the buzzwords/lingo being used?

5.   *Who* is the kind of person your target companies are looking for? (What kinds of values, strengths, enthusiasms, and resources would a successful CAREERpreneur need to possess?)

6.   What type of pay are these positions commanding? How does this shift across sectors?

7.   What kind of work environment is painted?

   Once you have researched the kinds of jobs you have typically searched for, see what happens when you search with your "green goggles" on.

8.   What pops up when you throw "sustainable," "conservation," "green," "environmental," and similar adjectives in front of your usual search terms? (e.g., conservation management, green customer service, environmental city planner, etc.)

Questions for Reflection

What are the 3 most important things you have learned from your research?

If you have identified gaps between what you bring to future opportunities and the actual opportunities that exist, what can you do to make yourself more competitive? (Ideas may include volunteering for an organization where target company members are likely to work, taking an online course or enrolling in a certificate program at a local university, or joining a professional membership organization to network with professionals and leaders in the field.)

Who (e.g., type of employer, sector, industry, size of company) is going to need what you do most and pay you what you are worth?

The Top 4 Growth Fields

While many of the jobs Pink eludes to when discussing the Conceptual Age will revolve around the green economy, some will simply complement it. These fields include:

1. **Healthcare**

   There are approximately 70-80 million Baby Boomers who have and will continue to transition into their older adult years over the next decade. Similarly, the oldest members of the 80-90 million member Generation Y, also referred to as Millennials, are entering into the family phase of their lives. This means that geriatric care and gynecology/family medicine will be two key fields and health professionals including doctors, nurses, occupational and physical therapists, and laboratory/medical technicians will continue to find lasting employment.

2. **Education**

   This field continues to thrive in almost any economy. There is frequently a teaching shortage in public and private primary and secondary education. There will also continue to be tremendous growth in alternative, charter and magnet schools, colleges and universities, continuing education, and adult education. Teachers, lecturers, and professors with expertise in areas with increased job growth (e.g., medicine, social services, computers, and environmental science) will naturally be most in need. When thinking about education, it is wise to remember the range of non-teaching positions that support classroom work including administrators, curriculum specialists, student development/leadership professionals, and athletic coaches.

3. **Social Services**

   As America and her sister nations continue to rebound from recession, it will take a range of professionals to ensure that the latest crises in our social, economic, and environmental landscape are footnotes in history rather than reoccurring themes. Social workers, psychologists, marriage and family therapists, addiction counselors, workforce trainers and specialists, and conflict mediators will therefore find employment working for federal, state, city and county agencies, nonprofit organizations, and in the education system.

4. Computer Software

In order for the range of technology we rely on to innovate—be it electronics, energy, or anything else—computer technology must evolve alongside it. Software engineers, IT analysts, web designers, and new media consultants will continue to be in high demand for as long as we continue to run on and consume technological products and services.

SUCCESSwork: When It Works, Repeat It

Directions: Pick a minimum of two of the four fields above to guide another round of print and online job research. Use the questions from *Know What's Out There.* Pay particular attention to #8 and substitute "green" and other similar adjectives for buzzwords appropriate to the field under investigation (e.g., social services administrator or health insurance computer engineer).

Questions for Reflection
What are the 3 most important things you have learned from your research?

If you have identified gaps between what you bring to future opportunities and the actual opportunities that exist, what can you do to make yourself more competitive? (Ideas may include volunteering for an organization where target company members are likely to work, taking an online course or enrolling in a certificate program at a local university, or joining a professional membership organization to network with professionals and leaders.)

Who (e.g., type of employer, sector, industry, size of company) is going to need what you do most and pay you what you are worth?

Next week, as we move into the *Building My Network* section, we will be exploring personal branding. Through your SUCCESSwork you will have an opportunity to identify what your brand is, how to develop it, and how to ensure that it stays authentic and "sticky."

Throughout the CAREERpreneurship process, it's important to take stock of what you have achieved and where you want to continue to focus your efforts to ensure you are getting your learning aims met and translating your insight into action.

SUCCESSwork: Phase 1 Reflection

Directions: As you did in Chapter 3, bring yourself back to that physical environment where whole body reflection can take place. Make sure that the following questions and your answers to previous SUCCESSwork are in tow. Take some time to release any tension you might be holding in your body. Bring your awareness to your breath, and take some nice, deep inhalations and exhalations. Once you have had some delicious moments of relaxation, muse on the following questions. Record your answers so that you can continue to track and celebrate your progress!

1. What are the Top 3 ways you have strengthened your personal foundation?

    _____

    _____

    _____

2. What has been the impact of adopting a CAREERpreneur's mindset over the last 4 chapters on yourself and those in your professional and personal life?

    _____

    _____

    _____

3. Where is there additional room for learning and growth?

_____

_____

_____

_____

_____

4. What SUCCESSwork will you give yourself around personal foundation to propel yourself towards a 10 (a Mastro's Steakhouse soufflé, or whatever that means for you)?

_____

_____

_____

_____

_____

5. How has your professional vision of *who* you want to be, *what* you want to be doing, and *how* you will be showing up to opportunities evolved?

_____

_____

_____

_____

_____

Part II

BUILDING MY NETWORK

Chapter Five

What Does My Brand Communicate?

For the next four chapters, we will be investigating the fundamentals of building a network of people who can help connect you to the professional opportunities you seek. During this time, we will explore the key players on a successful networking team (and how to find them). You will define your Unique Benefits Statement (UBS), craft it into a memorable 15-30 second introduction, come up with a customized and adaptable Paragraph of Introduction to use with the people you want to connect with, and of course, keep all of your CAREERpreneur success engineering grounded in your personal foundation.

First, we will start with the source of an effective networking strategy, YOU. You will devise key questions for identifying your authentic brand, the kind of impression you make on others, and how to ensure that who you are is "sticky" in the right way.

What Do You Mean I'm a *Brand*?

Dan Schawbel, the leading personal branding expert on Generation Y/Millennials says, *"Personal branding is about unearthing what is true and unique about you and letting everyone know about it."* While many people, me included, may not be keen on seeing ourselves as brands, Dan reminds us that branding is not *"a form of shameless self-promotion.... Developing your brand makes you a more valuable asset, whether to the company you work for, a potential employer, or your own enterprise."* In other words, personal branding is about giving rather than manipulating or taking.

Once you know how to articulate and share what makes you-you and how you are uniquely poised to provide solutions to companies and clients that need them and will compensate you well for them (Don't worry, we'll come back to this second idea in future chapters), then you can efficiently and creatively get yourself in front of the right people and make an impact.

In Dan's book, which all CAREERpreneurs should have on their shelves, *Me 2.0: Build a Powerful Brand to Achieve Career Success*, he says that the foundation of a brand is authenticity, or who you are at your core when all the bells and whistles are taken off.

SUCCESSwork: Unlocking Brand Irresistible YOU

Whenever I work with a client on branding, I always begin by asking a series of questions in 3 areas—Work, Style, and Self. These provide a nice gateway into the branding process.

Directions: Answer the questions below. Record your answers so that you can continue to pull from them as you hone in on your brand in the forthcoming SUCCESSwork for the chapter and as you develop your networking tools in chapters to come.

1. What do you do best? (Think about your specific tasks/those ES's you identified in Chapter 3)

    _____

    _____

    _____

2. How can you prove it? (Show vs. Tell)

_____

_____

_____

_____

_____

3. Who needs you most? Why?

_____

_____

_____

_____

4. What are the problems your prospective clients/companies have?

_____

_____

_____

_____

5. How do you provide a needed solution to them?

_____

_____

_____

_____

What is your favorite...

1. Taste?

_____

_____

_____

2. Scent?

_____

_____

_____

3. Tactile sensation?

_____

_____

_____

4. Physical environment?

_____

_____

_____

5. Music/Sounds?

_____

_____

_____

SELF

1. What brands (think of people, products, and services) get you jazzed? Why?

   _____

   _____

   _____

2. What are your core values?
   (Refer back to Week 3)

   _____

   _____

3. If your brand is a mirror for who you are, what would it reflect? (Is this what you want it to reflect?)

   _____

   _____

   _____

4. If your colleagues, friends, and family were to describe you in 3 adjectives, what would they be?

   _____

   _____

   _____

5. How do other people *feel* when they are around you?

   _____

   _____

   _____

Questions for Reflection

What are the top three discoveries you have made about your personal brand?

Based on these discoveries, how would you describe your brand? (Aim to do this in 2-3 sentences.)

What habits that you have created best share your brand with others? (e.g., a customized email signature or a phrase/mantra you often use)

What habits are not serving your brand well and need to be eliminated? (e.g., apologizing for no reason or having typos in emails)

In order for you to double the positive impact of your brand, what would need to occur?

SUCCESSwork: How Do Others Interpret Your Brand?

Although many of us are pretty good at identifying how others see us, most of us can still use a studio audience from time-to-time to double-check our self-impressions.

Directions: Connect with someone you don't know (or don't know very well) over the next week. Supermarkets, banks, professional networking events, parks, and public transportation are just a few of the places this can be done. **Inform this person that you are interested in getting his or her first impression. Ask the person how she or he would answer each of the following prompts about you.**

You come from _____.

Your career entails _____.

For fun, you enjoy _____.

Your greatest achievement is _____.

I should remember you because _____.

If this activity brings a little sweat to your upper lip, good! It means you are stepping outside of your comfort zone which will help you get ready for the weeks ahead when you will start reaching out to other professionals and thought leaders.

After you survive going through this activity once, consider doing it several more times to discover further the kind of first impression you paint. Remember, we all use prejudice (making an assumption before all facts are known) to make interpretations of the thousands of people, places, and things we encounter each day. The sooner you know how others prejudge you, the more quickly and accurately you can work on shaping and adjusting your brand.

Questions for Reflection

What did you discover about the first impression(s) you create?

How did your description of your brand compare or contrast to the descriptions of others?

What adjustments to your brand do you want to make based on the information you have obtained?

The "Sticky" Factor

In their book, *Made to Stick: Why Some Ideas Survive and Others Die*, authors Dan and Chip Heath describe stickiness as the ability to be understood, remembered, and have a positive lasting impact on your audience's thinking and behavior. For CAREERpreneurs, there is perhaps nothing more important than being sticky.

A 2007 Jobweb.com survey indicated that employers receive an average of 73 applications for each available entry-level position (MonsterTRAK).

Given that only 3-5 people are typically called in for an interview, and about the same number of companies or consultants are considered for providing a product or service, stickiness is going to determine whether you get a second glance or get thrown in the trash (or recycling bin if the person or company is environmentally-friendly!). Fortunately, there are only six principles to master.

The 6 Principles of Stickiness

1. Simplicity

Get to the heart of your message. How can you boil each idea you want to communicate down to one sentence?

2. Unexpectedness

As humans we tend to tune out what is familiar. In addition to defying expectations, how can you make an audience curious and eager to learn more?

3. Concreteness

People think in specifics and in images. How can you ensure that everything you say is NOT open to interpretation and instead evokes a clear and accurate picture?

4. Credibility

While some people like facts and statistics, most of us make choices based on whether we believe someone is qualified to give us what we want and need. How can you make credibility about your audience and not about you?

5. Emotions

If you want people to take action, ensure that your message strikes a personal chord with them. What is the emotion you are trying to evoke in order to spark the response you are looking for? (And here's a hint: *fear* is the LEAST compelling reason to make a decision or a purchase.) You want people to act because they are motivated by the result their choice is likely to produce.

6. Stories

I don't like to play favorites, yet I'd be duplicitous if I didn't share that this is by far my favorite sticky concept! Stories enable us to personalize the meaning we are trying to share. They can accomplish all of the other sticky principles, except perhaps the first one, by seamlessly drawing an audience in through their various senses. They are particularly invaluable in face-to-face networking, interviews, and even cover letters. What stories can you tell that will accomplish numbers 2-5?

SUCCESSwork: Applying Stickiness to Your Brand

Now, it's time to play with the principles of stickiness and make them work for your brand!

One's personal brand is determined by everything that is…

- A) <u>Said</u> (And *how* it is communicated)
- B) <u>Performed</u> (Ongoing behaviors as well as specific actions)
- C) <u>Seen</u> (Appearance in person, on the page, and online)
- D) <u>Associated with You</u> (Colleagues, friends, and family and ideas and concepts)

Directions: Pick one of the elements of personal branding lettered above. Identify the top three ways you communicate this component of your brand.

For example, when I do this exercise, I might pick "D." If I were to think about the Top 3 people or things associated with me, they would be:

- 1) CAREERpreneurship
- 2) Millennials/Generation-Y
- 3) Yoga and Meditation

Now, using the 6 Principles of Stickiness, identify The Top 10 Ways you can make this information about your brand "stick" for your target audience(s) (e.g., an HR manager or a small business owner you are looking to partner with). Be specific. Identify both the strategy you will use to defy expectations and the content it will contain (Principle 2). Actually write out and rehearse your story (Principle 6). See if you can use each sticky factor AT LEAST once.

The Top 10 Ways to Make My Brand Stick

1. _____

2. _____

3. _____

4. _____

5. _____

6. _____

7. _____

8. _____

9. _____

10. _____

Questions for Reflection

Which sticky principles did you most enjoy playing with? Why?

How can you continue to incorporate the sticky principles with the other facets of your personal brand?

How will you continue to assess how your personal brand is being received and remembered?

Moving forward, keep your eyes peeled for how you are forming your impressions of personal, product, and service brands. What sparks and holds your interest? What feels gimmicky or unappealing? How can you keep incorporating your impressions into your own brand development and maintenance?

In the next chapter, SUCCESSwork will focus on how to build a robust network of people who can best support you in climbing from your calling to your career. For it to be of maximum value, have your address book handy!

Chapter Six

Who's on My Team?

I n the last few chapters, we've focused on improving your own performance. This week we are going to shift gears to ensure that you surround yourself with greatness in the form of an All-Star Team. As a proud member of the self-empowerment movement, it saddens me to have to admit that we motivational folks can overemphasize working on the self and forget to encourage our followers to cultivate a community of like-minded people. Such self-centeredness, while useful in moderation, needs to take into account the myriad research that suggests we need to be engaged in meaningful work and in meaningful relationships to derive peak satisfaction from our lives. In this chapter, you are going to learn about each of the different roles that needs to be filled on your personal All-Star Team, identify who you know that can fill these positions, and brainstorm people you don't know, want to introduce yourself to, and by the end of the book *will* have connected with!

In *Who's Got Your Back: The Breakthrough Program to Build Deep, Trusting Relationships That Create Success and Won't Let You Fail*, author Keith Ferrazzi accredits his ability to build an "inner circle" of thought leaders and professionals for his sustainable success. He identifies four key ways that these kinds of "lifeline" relationships are beneficial:

1. To help us define what success means for us throughout the course of our careers.
2. To support us in developing our professional vision and corresponding short and long term goals to get us there.

3. To help us let go of the habits that hold us back and get us back on track for the success we deserve.

4. To connect with people who motivate us through their example to be the best version of ourselves each day of our lives.

Perhaps you're thinking, *"Don't you do those things for me, Alexia?"* And yes, a coach or expert can absolutely support you in the above ways. However, when you have additional people on your team in the following specific roles, you exponentially increase your professional success because each person brings a different vantage point and set of experiences to the playing field.

Engineering the All-Star Team

> *"Just think of how complicated and truly magnificent a human being is. When you think of all we are capable of—being able to love each other, and being willing to do something good in the world for no recognition . . . I am not saying there are not people who want to step over each other, who want to maim and kill, but that is a perversion of the beautiful things human beings are made for."* (Toni Morrison)

One of my mentors, happiness guru, author, and speaker Gabrielle Bernstein, loves to tell me to identify who has what I want and then hang out with those people, do what they do, and be of service to them. From Gabby I have learned so many CAREERpreneurship fundamentals, from the importance of always having a team (be they volunteers, interns, or paid staff) as the microphone for my message to always being clear on my two steps-ahead (and putting representations of those places on my vision board while staying open to the possibilities for how they will manifest). The best part about Gabby, beyond her effervescent spirit and commitment to changing the world, is that she is just one member of my All-Star Team. While no CAREERpreneur's team will look the same, there are some key roles that they have filled. They include:

1. **Cheerleaders**

   Cheerleaders are people who are going to remind you of the value you bring to others. They help you focus on your strengths. They enable you to show up to each day of your life at 100% so that you can play at 100%.

2. **Connectors**

   Connectors are people who enjoy opening their very full "little black books" to ignite mutually beneficial relationships between people. Not only do they know throngs of people, often across industries, they also are held in high regard because they do such a good job of playing professional matchmaker.

3. **Mentors**

   Mentors are typically veteran leaders in your field or a complementary one. They support you in developing your career through sharing what they have learned and how they have journeyed to their success. They may also help you with setting and achieving goals and developing the skills that are necessary for launching to the next level of success.

4. **Decision Makers**

   Decision makers are people who can actually give you opportunities, usually because they are in a position to hire you or give you business. In some cases they might be such experienced leaders that they supervise directly or indirectly the folks who make these decisions, and therefore they can ensure you are getting the consideration and face time you deserve.

Now that you understand the roles you will be filling, and please keep in mind they are not mutually exclusive (e.g., many cheerleaders are connectors), we will explore places you likely will be pulling your All-Star Team members from.

Alumni- These are people you met in college, graduate, or a professional school. This category also includes distinguished graduates you did not have a personal relationship with who nevertheless might take an interest in you given your shared alma mater.

Board Directors- These folks who serve on boards usually not only have power in the organization they are serving (be it in the corporate or nonprofit sector); they also typically hold influential positions within their own companies and in their communities.

Community Leaders- As the name suggests, these are revered people in your city or neighborhood. They may be elected officials, directors of government, nonprofit or community organizations, or leaders who have their feet in a lot of different professional groups and committees (e.g., Chamber of Commerce, Rotary Club, Kiwanis Club, etc.).

Experts- Every industry has people who are its go to speakers, writers, and commentators. These people can be found in bookstores, on the radio and TV, and giving keynotes at professional conferences and conventions. Almost all of them have websites, blogs, and various online networking profiles.

Hiring Managers- These are the people you interview with if you pass through the first level of review by Human Resources. They are usually the people who will hire and supervise you and are therefore typically middle managers within a department.

Human Resources Directors- In order to get to the Hiring Manager, you have to make it through Human Resources. Directors, managers, and their associates are going to screen through applications looking for position requirements and recommend the few people they perceive as the most experienced to the appropriate Hiring Manager. Remember, they are not experts in your field or role. They recommend candidates that best mirror what Hiring Managers state they are looking for.

Professors/University Administrators- Many of these folks have held or continue to hold significant positions in the private sector. They also might serve on influential boards and have relationships with alumni who are now working in your field. Consider connecting with university personnel from your alma mater(s) as well as at institutions in the community where you now reside or want to move to.

Recruiters- Unlike an employment agency that is going to place temporary, seasonal, and lower-skilled support staff in primarily clerical positions, recruiters are often industry specific and are on the hunt for professionals, managers, and executives for their high-profile clients. They are only going to select talent they feel their clients will be interested in (for they get paid and re-hired for making successful placements). If and when they do submit you, you will be considered more thoroughly than if you were to apply via a traditional application process. (Hint: If you are still a college student, make sure that you check-in with your campus employment center to see what recruiters will be coming to your campus. This is a great way to get in the door with a prestigious company.)

Thought Leaders- These are the people who are seen as innovators in their field. They are shaping the direction of their industry's ideas, often through the same channels as industry experts, but are always ten steps ahead rather than right on the pulse.

Family and Friends- And last, and most certainly not least, don't forget the people who are often the closest to you—who think you are the greatest thing since text messaging and will likely be very enthusiastic about introducing you to everyone they know!

Keep in mind that everyone you have ever met, as well as everyone that they have ever met, is a part of your network and a prospect for your All-Star Team. If you have not already created a system for storing business cards and contact information for the folks you meet, create one immediately. You never know when you or someone whose team you are on might want to reach out to that person. I won't tell you the dozens of people I have met and never stayed in touch with. Really, I won't. It's just too painful. It might make me develop shingles or…

Oh, all right. Let's just say one of them rhymes with Belinda Waites and another is currently the most powerful member of the Senate. A handful of these people are producers, directors, writers, and actors who collectively would probably have an EGOT (Emmy, Grammy, Oscar, and Tony). Hindsight is always 20-20; however, you can learn from my mistakes and both compile contact information from the people you meet and just as importantly, do a keen job of staying in touch with them.

SUCCESSwork: Designing the All-Star Team

In this chapter you have just one piece of SUCCESSwork because it is such an important one, and I want to make sure you give it your all. When you are thinking about who you want to bring onto your All-Star Team, the most important thing you can do is to believe in your ability to recruit anyone you identify as a good fit.

Don't worry about how you will connect to the person. I promise there is always a way, and you will develop your strategy in the weeks to come. For now, eliminate any glass ceiling you or others have created for your success, and think about who is necessary for getting you where you aspire to be. Then, make a note of them, and muse a bit on how you can provide value to them so that it's a mutually beneficial relationship you will ultimately propose you embark on together.

Directions: Create for yourself an All-Star Team that has each of the following roles filled. List the person's name (e.g., Hilda Hernandez) or her role if you are not yet sure of her name (e.g., Director of Community Relations at ABC Media). Under category, note which of the places listed above you pulled this person from (e.g., college alumni, recruiter, childhood friend, etc.). Pull from multiple places to increase your reach.

CHEERLEADERS

Name: _____

Category: _____

Name: _____

Category: _____

Name: _____

Category: _____

CONNECTORS

Name: _____

Category: _____

Name: _____

Category: _____

Name: _____

Category: _____

MENTORS

Name: _____

Category: _____

Name: _____

Category: _____

Name: _____

Category: _____

DECISION MAKERS

Name: _____

Category: _____

Name: _____

Category: _____

Name: _____

Category: _____

Questions for Reflection

Which of these people do you already have established relationships with?

Who are the people you don't know and want to? What will be the specific benefit of bringing them onto your team?

Who are the people you want on your team beyond *what* they do and *how* they can help you?

How might you be able to provide value to the team members you will eventually be reaching out to?

Resist the temptation to reach out to the people you have identified this week. We're going to be looking at how to make a dynamic, sticky first and follow-up impression over the next few chapters. Stay in the vision space for now. Get clear on who your All-Star Team players will be, how you will foster and maintain each relationship, and how you might be able to get in touch with people you don't yet know (e.g., through other team members, blogs, websites, online media, etc.). Consider placing these people on your vision board to reinforce your commitment to connecting with them. I have a big picture of one of my literary heroes, whose best-selling book we'll call *Sweet, Sashay, Shove* on mine. And there is not a doubt in my mind we will connect soon, and I suspect may already have by the time you are reading this sentence!

Chapter Seven

My First 15-30 Seconds

"*Hello. My name is _____. What do you do?*" I used to enjoy this question as much as an upper respiratory infection. Whether my answer was "*career coach,*" "*manager of a professional development program,*" or when my equal parts humorless and self-righteous co-Most Outstanding College of Liberal Arts Graduate asked me this question at our award ceremony and I responded, "*sex worker,*" (I was unsuccessful in eliciting so much as a flinch), I never took much pleasure in my answer. Once I stopped defining myself by job title, however, I had a lot more fun and started connecting successfully with the people who asked the question.

First impressions get a lot of lip service. And they should because they are important. However, the real question should not be, "*Is the impression I'm making a good one?*" but rather "*Am I making any impression at all?*"

Please understand, I'm not suggesting as so many Hollywood personalities and their agents and publicists seem to think that any press is good press. It's just that I've seen so many talented CAREERpreneurs focus on trying to present themselves the way they think others want them to show up that they wind up disappearing from memory and having to re-introduce themselves and make their first impression again and again.

Authenticity, as we've explored previously, is vital in your branding. However, just as theatre, TV, and film should be a more polished version of everyday conversation, your impression should be a slightly gussied up version of who you are. Therefore, we are going to take a look at how to put together language that states clearly who you are, the benefits you are uniquely poised to deliver, and develop your confidence so that *who* you are is reflected in *what* you say.

When you are thinking about the impressions you cast on others, consider the following:

The Top 10 Areas That Impact an Impression

1. The items you wear (e.g., clothing, accessories, shoes, piercings, and tattoos)
2. The language that you use and your delivery of it
3. Your online networking (e.g., Facebook, Twitter, LinkedIn, etc.)
    We will discuss these in more depth in Chapter 10.
4. Your email (the actual address, which should be professional, and the content of your messages)
5. Your blog and comments on other blogs
6. Your search engine footprint (Do pages show up and do they reflect you the way you want to be reflected?)
7. Your ratio between talking and listening (Do you ask more questions about the other person than you talk about yourself?)
8. Your ratio between taking value and providing value (Do you support others or simply ask them to support you?)
9. Accessible testimonials and endorsements (Can you prove that you are credible?)
10. Your confidence in who you are, what you do, and how you do it

Look over these ten areas, as well as your SUCCESSwork from Chapter 5. What do you discover about the impression of yourself that you are conveying to others?

Where are you strong?

Where is there some room for refinement?

What are you committed to doing to strengthen your impression?

SUCCESSwork: Your Unique Benefits Statement

A Unique Benefits Statement (UBS):

- Identifies specifically, in the first person, the results that you have delivered (and can deliver)
- How you impact your target market
- Is ONE sentence
- Uses an accurate and engaging verb (e.g., solve, heal, launch, strengthen)
- May change depending on who you are speaking with

I have three UBS that shift depending on whether I'm wearing my career or leadership hat or, as you will see from my first UBS, a combination of both. They are:

1) I empower leaders to build careers and companies that achieve what I have called the 3 S's: success, sustainability, and a positive social impact.

2) I devise innovative strategies for CAREERpreneurs looking to stand out in today's competitive marketplace and climb from their calling to their career.

3) I partner with companies and professionals who want to effectively market to, recruit, retain, and manage Millennials/Generation-Y's.

Directions: Create your own UBS using the template below. Strive to create at least 3: one that you can use with everybody and the others for two distinct ways you provide solutions that are needed (and will be well compensated). Refer to the values, strengths, enthusiasms, and resources discoveries you made in Chapter 3 for ideas.

> **I (powerful verb) for (clear target population) to (achieve a specific, desired result).**

Note: It may take you several permutations to hit upon the language that you like. As you are tinkering with your ideas, see what happens when you substitute verbs, weed out words you don't need, and speak your language out loud. You want to make sure that each of your UBS you can say clearly and in one breath.

My Unique Benefits Statements

_____

_____

_____

_____

_____

Questions for Reflection
We are going to hold off on processing the UBS since it is the foundation for your next SUCCESSwork. So just keep hanging in there with me.

SUCCESSwork: The 15-30 Second Pitch

Now that you have your UBS, you just have to add a few phrases to have your pitch. Many, like your name, you already know.

Start with <u>your introduction (your name and role, the latter only if you have one),</u> [stick in your UBS], add <u>a BRIEF statement of who or what you are looking for,</u> and follow-up with <u>a dynamic question to engage the person you are speaking with and help her to help you</u>. (Your question, like your UBS, will change depending on WHO you are speaking with and WHAT you are seeking to gain from the exchange.)

Here is the 15-30 second pitch that I frequently use when speaking with managers who supervise a large number of young employees.

Introduction: My name is Alexia Vernon and I am the Owner of Catalyst for Action.

UBS: I partner with companies and professionals who want to effectively market to, recruit, retain, and manage Millennials/Generation-Y's.

Who/What I'm Looking For: I am looking to connect with senior managers who want to meet their young employees where they are at and take them where they need to be.

> **Dynamic Question:** What would be the impact of having your youngest employees become your top performers?
>
> **Putting It All Together:** My name is Alexia Vernon and I am the Owner of Catalyst for Action. I partner with companies and professionals who want to effectively market to, recruit, retain, and manage Millennials/Generation-Y's. I am looking to connect with senior managers who want to meet their young employees where they are at and take them where they need to be. What would be the impact of having your youngest employees become your top performers?

Why is it important to end with a question? Well, as you can probably see, if your question is one that allows the people you are speaking with to imagine a problem being solved or envision their next level of success, they are going to have a favorable impression of you and also want to hear how you possess the tools to make what they seek happen.

Directions: It's your turn! Using the template and example of a 15-30 second pitch above, create your own. Remember that you will probably want a few models and that really, each time you speak your pitch will come out a little differently. **For now, try to come up with one for a potential employer and one for a prospective member of your All-Star Team.**

My 15-30 Second Pitches

Questions for Reflection

Who do you envision delivering your pitches to?

What will be the likely responses? What do you need to have prepared for them?

How do your pitches set you apart from your competition?

What happens when you try out your pitches on friends and family? What lands well for them? What needs to be adjusted?

Fierce Presentations

One of my guilty pleasures *was*—notice my intentional use of the past tense for I've been clean three seasons—watching Tyra Banks' *America's Next Top Model*. The best thing to come out of that show is Tyra's concept of *fierce*. To my knowledge Tyra never defines it. However, the essence of the idea is showing up to fear-inducing situations with *chutzpah* (which, for my readers without a trace of Jewish blood running through them, means a fusion of courage and confidence).

In order for you to make the impact you desire on your All-Star Team, a prospective employer or client, or anyone else you meet, it is vital that you show up *fierce*. And *fierce* takes a lot of practice before it becomes habitual (as evidenced by some of Tyra's models who never seemed to figure out how to wear three-inch heels and a micro-mini while sashaying down a runway). Fortunately for you, your rehearsal of *fierce* is free of any movement restricting accoutrement!

For several years while negotiating my shift from employee to CAREERpreneur, I taught public speaking to college students. And I am distilling my 16-week course down into:

The Top 10 Principles You Need to Know to Give a *Fierce* Presentation

1. **Public speaking is Americans' number 1 fear.** (Death is number 2). Remember that fear is normal AND surmountable.

2. **For each minute you speak, you want to practice 1-2 hours.** (This is to enable you to transcend fear so that you can get to *fierce* AND know exactly how you will accomplish your aims).

3. **Each time you speak and want the person or people listening to take action, it's a persuasive speech.** Therefore, you must draw your audience in, state clearly where you are going to go, deliver the argument (a mix of main and supporting points, examples, and most importantly stories and entertainment) necessary for them to understand your perspective and take action, re-cap the guts of what you've just done, and leave your audience clear on why they must take action NOW. This last step is known as a call-to-action.

    Note: The longer that people wait to make a decision, the less likely it is that they will. In her breathtaking book on speaking before potential clients and small and large groups for maximum impact, *New Sales Speak: The 9 Biggest Sales*

Presentation Mistakes and How to Avoid Them, Terri Sjodin explains that even if you give an effective presentation, have compelling points, skillfully summarize your argument in your conclusion, and make a clear call-to-action, people forget 50% of what they've just heard immediately after. Then, after another 10 minutes, they lose another 10%. By the time they get home, another 10%. And by the next day, yet another 10% evaporates. So if you follow-up two-days after you spoke, that person has likely remembered, at best, 20% of your message.

Make sure that when you want something specific from an audience, whether it is an audience of 1 or 1,000, that you make an appeal so compelling you are justified in asking for an answer on the spot. If for any reason that just isn't possible, set a mutually agreed upon time and place (if face-to-face) for a follow-up conversation. And don't allow too much time to elapse before the date.

4. **How you deliver your information is as important, if not more so, than what you are saying.** One of my generational expert colleagues, Cam Marston, recently shared with me that when he started his professional speaking career one of his advisors told him, *"Make sure that 80% of what you do is entertain. That's what the audience will remember."* It's as important to spend time on *how* you present your material as it is on *the message* you seek to transmit.

5. *Show* **rather than** *tell.* While you want to give facts to support your claims (e.g., I saved my last company $2000 in one month by implementing a new expense tracking system or I sold $25,000 of product in my first six months), what the person listening to you is going to connect with is a compelling story. As we discussed in Chapter 5 while exploring the concept of "sticky," have well rehearsed stories at your disposal to illustrate and, when necessary, prove your points. And follow the advice of Cam's advisor. Make sure they are entertaining.

6. **People like to laugh as much as possible.** And nobody I know has ever claimed she or he laughs too much! According to Gretchen Rubin, the author of *The Happiness Project*, while children laugh an average of 400 times per day, adults laugh just an average of 17. Ensure that you are someone who gives each audience a good time and gets them above that disappointing average adult daily laugh rate.

7. **Physical appearance (revisit *The Top 10 Areas that Shape an Impression*) and body language matter.** Not only should you practice before others. You should also consider taping yourself in the clothing you plan to wear to speak, interview, etc. to identify and fix awkward articles and accessories, facial expressions, or gestures. Nobody will be as rigorous with feedback (unless you hire a speaking coach) as you.

8. **Each audience is different.** Make sure you know *who* you are speaking with and adapt (e.g., dress, examples, and other features of delivery) to meet them where they are at. Communication must be audience-centered for it to have a positive impact.

9. **Great speakers are great listeners.** When you listen well, you are able to hear and anticipate the verbal and non-verbal feedback an audience will give, and you can strategize comebacks to likely objections. Start taking note of how well you retain what others are saying to you. When someone asks you a question, do you answer it? When you speak, is it about you or about the person you are engaging with?

10. **Speaking is like any muscle. Use it or lose it.** If you challenge yourself to initiate conversations that push you outside your comfort zone, introduce yourself to new prospects, and speak publicly on a regular basis, you will need less and less preparation. However, if this is something you only do from time-to-time, be prepared to continue giving a lot of your attention, energy, and time to it so that you can show up *fierce*.

SUCCESSwork: The *Fierce* Daily Habit

Before you begin sharing your 15-30 second pitch with others, (which you will be charged to do in the next chapter), it's important to start flexing your *fierce* muscle so that you don't waste any potential opportunity by giving a lackluster presentation.

Directions: Identify a daily activity that you do (e.g., brushing your teeth, making your bed, cleaning dishes, etc.). **Create a 2-3 minute <u>persuasive</u> presentation (following ALL of the 10 principles above) to convince an audience that your method for performing the habit should be applied by them. After you have perfected your presentation, perform it for an audience and, if possible, tape it so that you can review and learn from it.**

Questions for Reflection

What did you discover about your persuasive speaking abilities? What do you want to keep and what do you want to chuck into the trash?

How long did you have to practice to get to *fierce*?

What are your natural stylistic elements? (For me, they include silly multiple-choice quizzes, Top 10 lists, asking for audience input, and quirky hand and corresponding face gestures.) How can you incorporate your productive stylistic elements into your networking, pitching, and speaking?

When you revisit your 15-30 second pitch, what adjustments can you make to ensure it allows you to be as *fierce* as possible?

I imagine that at this point you need to take some deep breaths. Please do so. Take a deep breath in, focusing on a word that summarizes what you most need from yourself right now (e.g., strength, calm, or chutzpah). And take a nice long exhale, releasing any limiting thoughts, feelings, or beliefs as you focus on a word that summarizes what you are contributing to the world (e.g., forgiveness, playfulness, aloha). Do this a few times, making sure that your breathing is full-bodied and your thoughts are directed just on your two words. Observe how your breath and intention on your words begins to impact the rest of your body.

I have given you A LOT to do and muse on. As you continue to hone your pitch and develop your ability to be a *fierce* communicator, stay on top of your personal foundation work. It will ensure that you have the goods to make CAREERpreneurship a way of *being* and not simply another theory that sounds good, yet never gets translated into action or habit.

Chapter Eight

My Second 15-30 Seconds

As you start building your All-Star Team, you will most likely be reaching out to people you do not have an established relationship with. Some of the people you reach out to will not be the right fit; however, they will likely refer you to people they know who can better give you what you want and need. You need to have a Paragraph of Introduction in your pocket to pull out anytime you want to plant the seed for a new relationship. This paragraph will be sent via email, or when you don't have the person's email address, LinkedIn *(which we will explore in Chapter 10)*.

Best Practices for Paragraphs of Introduction

1. **Introduce yourself by using your 15-30 second introduction.** (Hold off on asking your question).
2. **Explain why you are reaching out to this person and not somebody else.** (e.g., If somebody recommended that you reach out or you have read this person's column, blog, book, etc., you mention this early in the paragraph to establish rapport.)
3. **Make your ask.** What is it you want this person to do? (e.g., Meet with you face-to-face or on the phone, connect you to her hiring manager, provide an endorsement of your previous work, etc.)
4. **Communicate what you have to offer this person and your intention of fostering a mutually beneficial relationship.**

5. **Finally, you state that you will call them the next week.** And you do!

6. **Before you hit "send," proofread your paragraph.** Then, have a few sets of eyes that you trust proofread it for you. Then, and only then, are you ready to share it with the recipient.

Sample Paragraph of Introduction to an All-Star Team Member

Dear Ms. Lupa Campos,

My name is Wayne Jackson and I empower vulnerable communities to find solutions to systematic social, economic, and environmental injustice. I have been a huge fan of your environmental justice blog, *See No Evil, Continue the Evil*, since it was recommended to me as a graduate student at Pace University by Professor Thomas, a former colleague of yours. Because of your approximately twenty-five years of experience as a community organizer and now, state senator, I would love the opportunity to learn firsthand how you have brought your values, strengths, and enthusiasms to those who need you most. In addition, I would like to explore with you how I can best build a sustainable career in this important field. I'll be contacting you next week to schedule a mutually agreeable time for me to speak with you further.

Much thanks,
Wayne Jackson

SUCCESSwork: Create the Template for *Your* Paragraph of Introduction to All-Star Team Members

Directions: It's time to put the pedal to the metal! Create your template for the Paragraph of Introduction using the best practices and examples above. Then, identify at least 5 people you want to send it to and do it!

My Paragraph of Introduction

5 People to Send My Paragraph of Introduction

1. _____

2. _____

3. _____

4. _____

5. _____

Questions for Reflection

How does it feel to have the template for your Paragraph of Introduction completed?

What section(s) of the paragraph will be adjusted from one person to the next?

How will you create a schedule that allows you to reach out to the prospective members of your Team and follow-up with them while still negotiating your other professional and personal responsibilities?

SUCCESSwork: Pitching One Conversation at a Time

Directions: Identify at least 3 opportunities for yourself over the next week to practice your 15-30 second pitch. Consider reaching out to former classmates in your field or former co-workers. You can also attend a general community meeting (e.g., Chamber of Commerce, Rotary Club, or Kiwanis Club) or industry-specific networking meeting (e.g., your local chapter of American Society for Training and Development,

American Management Association, or Air and Waste Management Association). If unsure of opportunities, carve out some time for internet searching. Try putting in your city, state, your field, and then association (e.g., Nevada Professional Coaches Association). **Refer back to the principles of *fierce* communication we covered in the last chapter to ensure that each time you open your mouth you are speaking for maximum impact.**

Opportunities for Practicing My 15-30 Second Pitch

1. _____

2. _____

3. _____

4. _____

5. _____

6. _____

7. _____

8. _____

9. _____

10. _____

Questions for Reflection

What did you discover by sharing your pitch?

How did your prospects answer the question at the end?

Where were you most successful?

What do you want to continue to refine?

Following Up with a Prospect

As you start going out, getting yourself in front of people in your field, and delivering your 15-30 second pitch, it is important to follow-up with anyone you meet within 24-hours. As you learned last week, by the time you wait 48-hours, that person will only remember, at most, 20% of what you have said!

This Follow-Up Paragraph is going to have the same basic format as your Paragraph of Introduction. Your first two points, however, will be amended based on how much you previously got to know one another. Your overarching aim here is to find a time to meet so that you can either conduct an Informational Interview *(the focus of Chapter 9)* or more casually (perhaps over coffee) get to know one another better.

Sample Follow-Up Paragraph

Dear Raj,

I thoroughly enjoyed meeting you at last night's Young Professionals Mixer. As I shared with you during our brief chat, I have five years experience designing technology solutions for busy small business owners who'd rather work *in* their businesses than *on* their businesses. You mentioned that your company, E-Friendly Connections, is looking to expand its technology systems. I'd love to share with you some of the innovative programs I've designed in the past and explore how my skill set could be used to take your company to the next level of success. I'll be contacting you next week to schedule a mutually agreeable time for me to meet with you.

Much thanks,
Trisha Santiago

SUCCESSwork: The Follow-Up Paragraph

Directions: Create a sample Follow-Up Paragraph to send each person that you meet. Unlike your Paragraph of Introduction that stays relatively similar for each person you reach out to, your Follow-Up Paragraph needs to adapt to reflect the exchange(s) that you and this person have already shared. By completing the template below, you will at least get comfortable with the structure we just explored.

My Follow-Up Paragraph Template

continue on the next page

My Follow-Up Paragraph Template

Questions for Reflection

Are you sending your Paragraphs within 24-hours of meeting someone AND calling when you say you will to schedule a follow-up meeting or conversation?

How are your preparing for your meetings? Are you clear on what you want from the other person and making a specific and appropriate *ask*?

How is your confidence in yourself, as a communicator and professional who has value to deliver, evolving the more you present before others?

When you reach out to All-Star Team prospects as well as new and existing contacts you want to reconnect with, remember to be as specific as possible about what you are looking for and empower these people to help you.

Career coach and LYJ: Love Your Job, Love Your Life! Co-Founder Suzanne Grossman recommends the following:

Provide your network with a list of 5-10 companies that would be your dream location to work. *Paint a picture for your network of where you envision yourself. A recent contact sent around an email saying she was interested in positions in "the arts." This could mean any number of things. What does this mean to her? I asked her to send me a list of 5 dream companies, and she replied with museums and historical sites. Now I had a much better picture of what she had in mind. I also learned that she was looking to stay in the Washington, DC area, information that was not supplied in her original email.*

Do let your network know the department, division, and job title you envision yourself with. *Similar to letting your contacts know where you see yourself working, let them know in what role(s). For example, a large institution like NYU or any other major university has a communications staff, finance, fundraising, teaching roles, positions that involve more writing than others, working with students or not. What types of skills and experience do you have and what areas do you see yourself in? Also, are you looking only for full-time or are you open to part-time and freelance? Let your network know as best you can.*

As we transition into the third phase of the book, you will learn how informational interviews give you a reason to follow-up and present yourself before anyone you want. We will cover best practices for face-to-face and online networking, explore strategies for designing resumes and cover letters that land with a bang rather than a bust, investigate essentials for successful interviewing, build your platform as an expert in your field, and I promise there are oodles of other CAREERpreneurship goodies awaiting you. First, however, it is time for some cumulative reflection.

SUCCESSwork: Phase 2 Reflection

Directions: As you did in Chapters 3 and 4, bring yourself back to that physical environment where whole body reflection can take place. Make sure that the following questions and your answers to previous SUCCESS-work are in tow. Take some time to release any tension you might be holding in your body. Bring your awareness to your breath, and take some nice, deep inhalations and exhalations. Once you have had some delicious moments of relaxation, muse on the following questions. Record your answers so that you can continue to track and celebrate your progress!

1. What are the Top 3 things you have learned about building a network of helpful people?

   _____

   _____

   _____

2. What has been the impact of adopting a CAREERpreneur's mindset over the last 4 chapters on yourself and those in your professional and personal life?

   _____

   _____

   _____

3. Where is there additional room for learning and growth?

    _____

    _____

    _____

4. What SUCCESSwork are you giving yourself around personal foundation and building a network to increase your capacity for success?

    _____

    _____

    _____

5. How has your professional vision of *who* you want to be, *what* you want to be doing, and *how* you will be showing up to opportunities evolved?

    _____

    _____

    _____

Part III

THE CAREERPRENEUR'S ESSENTIAL TOOLS

Chapter Nine

The Why and How of Informational Interviewing

Let's kick-off with an important and sobering fact. Anywhere from 70-95% of jobs are obtained through networking. (Now, I hope you can understand my apprehension at relying on internet listings for jobs.) Having a full address book is not enough to be an effective CAREERpreneur. You need to understand how to empower your All-Star Team and the rest of your network to work for you!

In this first of the following eight chapters centered on *The CAREERpreneur's Essential Toolkit*, we will define informational interviews, investigate how they are important to developing a successful and sustainable career, and ensure that you have a strategy in place for leveraging them in your success engineering.

Informational interviews are hands-down my favorite way for CAREERpreneurs to take control of their career development. And fellow career experts agree…

"Informational interviews are one of the most powerful tools in your job hunting arsenal." (Heather Huhman, Founder of Come Recommended, career author, and columnist)

Informational interviews *"are a terrific entry point to establishing a potentially valuable long-term relationship."* (Alexandra Levit, workplace and career expert and author of such books as *New Job, New You, They Don't Teach Corporate in College*, and *Success for Hire*)

"I am a huge fan of informational interviews...Talking to people about their jobs and companies is a great way to (1) learn about people and organizations and (2) introduce yourself, your skills and accomplishments to people who will (hopefully) like you and want to help you with your plans." (Miriam Salpeter, Founder of Keppie Careers, career coach, and writer)

What is an *Informational Interview*?

An informational interview is an interview that you, as a CAREERpreneur, set and run with a professional or leader in your field to learn about that person's career development, company and to cast yourself as an important contributor to your field. You will request and conduct informational interviews with anyone you want to utilize as a member of your network, particularly prospective members of your All-Star Team: Cheerleaders, Connectors, Mentors, and especially Decision Makers.

There are 10 Steps to Maximizing the Informational Interview

1. **Score Face Time**

   You send your Paragraph of Introduction or Follow-Up Paragraph, as appropriate, following the steps we outlined in Chapter 8. You DON'T attach a resume, and you DON'T ask for a job.

   While job opportunities, business relationship, and clients often come out of informational interviews, this is not what informational interviews are for. Your goal should be to introduce a leader in your field to what you have done and what you plan to achieve next, learn as much as you can from this person's experiences, and make yourself so irresistibly attractive during the interview that the interviewee keeps his or her ear to the pavement for opportunities for you, many of which may actually be outside of the person's organization.

2. **Breathe and Then Bulldoze Forward**

You called your prospect when you said you would. And after a few rounds of phone tag, you have likely scheduled an informational interviewee. Most likely you have a week or so before your (hopefully face-to-face) meeting to prepare.

It's important to celebrate this victory and recognize that a little bit of smart work has paid off. After a night off, though, it's time to get back into preparation mode. So keep reading. (And remember to re-confirm your informational interview 24-hours before the appointment.)

3. **Design Your Strategy**

As you go through Step 3, make sure to have your SUCCESSwork from Chapter 5 handy. Identify *what* you seek to communicate by the end of the informational interview. Ideally, you should have three concrete things you want to leave your interviewee with. Then, work backwards and identify *how* you will ensure your goals are achieved.

Keep in mind that you are running this interview. You have the ability and the responsibility to design questions, pull together stories, and prepare answers that enable you to prove your value to your interviewee.

Make sure that you are practicing all of your interview facilitation OUT LOUD. While you want to sound natural, you still want to weed out vocalized thinking (e.g., um, you know, like, so, etc.) and know how and why you are transitioning from one point to the next.

4. **Be Curious**

In addition to planning what you want to communicate about yourself to the person you are speaking with, remember that this is an opportunity to learn and grow. Know what the heck it is you want to discover by the end of your informational interview and make sure that you have prepared questions that enable you to get the answers you seek.

There are oodles of great informational interview questions for free online. One of my favorite compilations is from Quintessential Careers (http://www.QuintCareers.com/information_interview.html).

I suggest customizing your questions to your particular industry and focusing them around five or six major themes (e.g., emerging trends in the field, recommended academic and experiential qualifications, opportunities for career advancement and learning, or workplace culture and values) rather than trying to cover dozens of different topics and jumping around from one category to another. This will enable you to walk away with a deeper understanding of your field and interviewee and show that you know how to create and adhere to a focused agenda.

One question I always recommend CAREERpreneurs ask if interested in working at the company of their informational interviewee is, *"Does your company have an employee referral program?"* (If the answer is yes, that means that if your informational interviewee recommends you for a position and you get hired, that person will receive some form of a compensation from the company as a thank-you.) Therefore, this question is as much about planting a seed as it is finding out the 411.

5. **Make Your Interviewee Comfortable**

    From the moment you step into the building where you are meeting your interviewee throughout the life of the relationship you are cultivating, you want your interviewee to share information that is really going to inform the development of your career. Regardless of the questions you ask, you want to encourage this person to talk about her or himself as much as possible. This will keep the interviewee engaged, and more importantly, enable you to get as much of an insider perspective on the job/field/business as possible. Ask for examples or stories to illustrate what your interviewee is stating. Unlike a job interview where you are on the hot seat, you are the host of this show. Make it fun for yourself and the interviewee, and solicit information you couldn't read in a book or on a website.

6. **Learn What Goes on Within a Company's Four Walls**

    Believe it or not, professional satisfaction is not solely about landing in an industry we find interesting. Rather, it's about consistently performing tasks that enable us to play to our strengths, engaging in meaningful relationships, and feeling like our work is making a positive and significant impact. It's no easy feat finding a work environment that enables us to thrive, even if we are in our own business. How can you ask questions that enable you to ascertain whether this type of company can provide what you desire—or whether your interviewee can provide leads to others that can?

7. *Share* Yourself

Given that you are reading this book, it's likely that you are conducting this informational interview because you'd like your next career move to enable you to advance to the next level of success, contribution, and happiness. You know this. And so does your interviewee. While you are not interviewing for a job and/or a client, you are sniffing around for opportunities the person sitting before you can help you land whether it is affiliated with his or her company or with someone he or she knows.

Give your informational interviewee both a reason and an opportunity to give you what you want. Find repeated reasons to tell your interviewee of your unique benefits and strengths. Share what you have previously achieved. Help the person imagine what new things you will accomplish when given the right opportunity. Have specific stories and examples rehearsed and at your disposal.

If you know this person can offer you something, gosh darn it, ask for it. And be specific. If you are hoping that she or he will be a member of an All-Star Team and be someone you can turn to for cheerleading, connecting, or one of the roles, let her or him know. If you sense that this person may not be the right fit, yet someone she or he knows might be, make your ask.

I once had an informational interviewer ask me to identify my three favorite coaches and make introductions to them for her. And I did. I'd much rather put myself on the line for someone who knows what she wants (e.g., for me to proofread a resume and cover letter, share my perception of her strengths and areas for growth, or serve as a mentor) rather than hem and haw over how to help someone who doesn't give me any parameters for how I can quickly be of use.

8. Solicit Feedback

Every informational interview is successful if you have learned something. One of the greatest gifts an interviewee can offer is feedback on how we can make ourselves more competitive to prospective employers and clients, one of which might be them. Ask if the interviewee will take a look at your resume, pitch, or make a recommendation for a course or hands-on learning opportunity. Two of my favorite feedback questions are:

"If I were applying for an open position in your company, what would be necessary for my application to POP for you?"

"If I were asking for your business, what would be necessary for you to say Yes right on the spot?"

9. **End with a Bang, NOT a Whimper**

This is one of the central tenets for giving a successful conclusion to a speech or presentation. It is also pivotal for bringing your informational interview to a strong close and ensuring it is the beginning rather than the culmination of a relationship.

First impressions are important; so are subsequent ones. When you are wrapping up with your interviewee (as the interviewer, you should have stayed within a mutually agreed upon time limit), you want to reinforce what makes you a standout from your competition (your UBS). Ask for permission to follow up with your interviewee. You also want to take this opportunity to ask if there is anything you can do to help. And if there is a particular role you are hoping this person will play in your career development, don't leave the interview without asking!

The platinum rule of networking is you have to give to receive. Showing that you are committed to investing in relationships, not just taking from them, will score you many bonus points.

10. **Find Reasons to Reconnect**

Send your email or handwritten thank-you note to your interviewee within 24-hours. Reflect on the experience and try to find a reason to be in touch within the next one to two weeks. And, particularly if you have asked and received permission to include this person as an All-Star Team member, continue to reconnect every six to eight weeks moving forward. If your interviewee is a member of any online or face-to-face social networks, blogs, or speaks live/has podcasts, join and participate in these activities. Also, consider forwarding articles the person will find of professional or personal interest.

Most importantly, remember that relationship building works best when we invest continuously in it and provide value to others. Continue to check out how you can provide value to this new or strengthened member of your network. Not sure what you have to offer? Ask!

A Success Story in Informational Interviewing

As we have previously explored, there are dozens of ways to find prospects for informational interviewing and for finding members for your All-Star Team:

- Connecting with professors and alumni from your alma mater or a local college
- Reaching out to previous co-workers and current colleagues in similar companies or professional associations
- Looking for experts and thought leaders with online articles, blogs, websites, or networking profiles on such sites as LinkedIn, Facebook, or Twitter. *(More information on maximizing online networking in Chapter 10)*

However, what happens when you have a loose idea of *who* you want to interview, yet you don't quite know *how* to make it happen? One CAREERpreneur shares how he used his detective skills to find his desired informational interviewee…. and a job!

When I relocated back to the city where I had graduated from college, I decided to take one of my old college friends out to lunch. My guiding question was simple. "Who is hiring in our field?" Of course, it wasn't just about finding out where opportunities were or who the Hiring Manager was at such-and-such company. It was about connecting with my friend and learning what he was up to; if he was looking for something specific, perhaps I could help him with his situation.

I was able to get a name of one company that sounded like a good fit. From there, I researched the company online and found out who was in charge nationally. The company's website had a great mission statement as well as useful information on their current projects, but there was only a general email address. Not good. I wanted to find a person in the local area who made the hiring decisions. Instead of going to my last resort of conducting a cold call to their local office, I decided to hit up some of the social networking websites. After registering on LinkedIn (Free!), I entered the company's name and my city. Lo and behold, I found someone who worked in the local office who was a Hiring Manager. Instead of requesting to be a part of his network on LinkedIn (which may take several weeks, depending on how often he checks the website, and he may decline my request since he doesn't know me), I decided to do more investigating. I had a name. My target was narrowing.

I cross-referenced the contact's name on Google, and I learned that my contact had earned his degree in civil engineering and was the Vice President of Transportation and Planning at the company—not exactly my interest. But if anyone could tell me the proper person to contact in my target department, it would be him. I researched city transportation planning boards and learned that my contact was on the Board of the City's Transportation Council. Because it's a public entity, they have to be transparent about who's on the council and where they live, and THAT'S where I found his contact information.

It might have been much easier to call the company directly, find out who was in charge, and ask for an informational interview. That could have taken 15 minutes to accomplish, and I would have been able to move on, assuming the first person that picked up the phone didn't hang up on me! My process took half a day, but it accomplished more than just finding contact information. I was able to find out what projects the company was doing and what organizations the company was a part of. I was able to convey in a very comprehensive manner why I wanted to interview my prospect. You see, it's not just because I wanted a job that I wanted to talk with this person. As I moved through my research, I saw a company that was savvy in social networking and was intentional in reaching out to diverse communities; this was a company that spoke to my core values.

After emailing, I followed up with a phone call. Unfortunately, my contact was not able to see me, but because I emailed him with my specific strengths, interests, and previous results delivered, he was able to give me the contact information of someone who makes the hiring decisions in my target department. I contacted this person, bribed her with lunch, and was able to get great suggestions on strengthening my candidacy for a position with the company, other people in the field to contact, and other companies who may be hiring.

So, did I get a job with this company? No....at least not yet. For I wound up being hired by a company a friend of a friend connected me with before this company was ready to take anyone on. While I love my current position, I know this company now knows my face and that I'm willing to go the extra step. (Such as taking staff out to lunch and conducting informational interviews...how many candidates actually do that?) When a position opens up with this company, they're looking forward to meeting with me again. They've said so! And if it allows me to step up from my current position, the best part is that I won't need to wait until I see the job opening online before applying, because by then it would be too late.

The definition of "career" comes from the Middle French word "carrier," meaning a course or road. Understanding that my career is my life's course and that a job is only part of this process assures me that I'm on my way!

SUCCESSwork: Running Knock-Out Informational Interviews

Directions: Using the *10 Steps to Maximizing the Informational Interview* detailed, make a plan for how you will use informational interviews as a CAREERpreneurship tool over the next 6 months. Work backwards.

Where do you want to be 6-months from now?
(e.g., have a full All-Star Team, land a full-time internship or job in my field, find my next big client, be on the Board of Directors of my professional organization)

_____

_____

_____

_____

Who do you need to meet and interview to make the goals a reality?

_____

_____

_____

_____

How can you set an aggressive and achievable timeline for setting up and conducting the necessary informational interviews over the next 6-months?

_____

_____

_____

_____

Questions for Reflection

(After each informational interview, consider the following):

Where did I excel in the informational interview?

Where did I not perform as well? How can I strengthen this area?

How did the informational interview enable me to take smart action toward my goals?

What did I learn that I will apply in future correspondence with this person and in future informational interviews?

What personal foundation areas do I want to re-visit and focus on so that I can show up to informational interviews at 100%?

Chapter Ten

Utilizing Online Media

While it is far easier to make a dazzling impression on a prospective employer, client, or All-Star Team member face-to-face, online media is still a worthwhile medium for establishing contact with professional peers, managers, and leaders. It is equally useful for searching for positions (assuming you are connected with the right folks) and for building on new and existing relationships.

This week we will explore my three top online media picks for CAREERpreneurs—LinkedIn, Twitter, and Facebook. While there are hundreds, possibly thousands of additional sites, you want to be where the people who can connect, employ you, and give you business flock. And currently, the three aforementioned sites are commanding the greatest professional traffic.

Online Media 101: A Survey Course for CAREERpreneurs

LinkedIn

LinkedIn (http://www.LinkedIn.com) is the largest online network for professionals. As of this printing, it has approximately 65 million members. It is also the MOST important because it allows CAREERpreneurs to post their resumes, connect with other professionals, compile recommendations, link to affiliated websites (e.g., other online media accounts, blogs, personal websites), ask questions, search for jobs, and even control their search engine results. Simply by setting up a LinkedIn account, you ensure that when anyone puts your name into a search engine, your LinkedIn profile will be one of the top items to appear.

The Top 10 Ways to Maximize LinkedIn

1. **Create a full-profile.** Make sure that you complete a full professional summary (your UBS or 15-30 second introduction), list your specialties (any key words or phrases a prospective employer, recruiter, or client would search for), your location, and your field. List all of your work, volunteer, and educational experiences (as you would on a chronological resume). Only link to websites that enhance your brand. And make sure that you include a professional looking picture. If you don't have a headshot, consider going outdoors and having a friend or loved one snap some shots in front of a simple backdrop; trees, mountains, and brick buildings work particularly well.

2. **Solicit recommendations.** You can both receive and give recommendations to any of your contacts—professors, colleagues, peers, clients, former classmates, supervisors, or managers. As a rule, you want to showcase between 3-5 recommendations to have a complete profile. When requesting recommendations from a contact, consider asking the person to use the following questions as a guide:

    In what capacity have we known one another?
    What specific results or solutions have you seen me deliver?
    Can you give an example of one of them?
    What else would you want a prospective employer, recruiter, or client to
        know about me?

3. **Use the search feature.** At the top of the website, you have the opportunity to search for many things, including people, jobs, companies, and groups. This is the key both to learning about existing opportunities and, more importantly, for building your contacts ideally to a minimum of 100 useful people. Quality not

quantity matters on LinkedIn. You are likely to achieve both if you are sending requests to connect to folks at companies and in groups in your interest area.

4. **Join as many relevant groups as you can and engage with the members.** Only allow the groups that most relate to your career and brand to be visible on your profile, and make sure that you select to have updates sent to you weekly rather than each time someone posts. Once you are a member of a group, you can send a request to connect to any of the members without knowing their email addresses AND you can read and respond to discussions, news, and jobs posted by them. So if you want to connect with someone and don't know the person's email address (a requirement for sending an invitation to connect if you did not previously work or attend school with the person), consider searching the person's group(s) and joining. Then, you will be able to send the invitation without knowing the email address!

5. **Personalize your requests to connect.** Use the template for your Paragraph of Introduction. Make it a habit to connect on LinkedIn with anyone you meet.

6. **Post status updates.** These should always be professional and show existing and prospective contacts that you are engaged in your field. Consider asking relevant questions here, in addition to in the search box, to encourage others to connect and converse with you. If you have a Twitter account, you can have your Twitter updates feed to your LinkedIn account.

7. **Participate in LinkedIn sponsored learning opportunities.** Through your online group membership you will have access to a lot of FREE or low-cost learning. Take advantage of these opportunities for professional development and make sure to participate, if possible, and connect after the learning programs with the facilitator(s) and other active participants.

    Lindsey Pollak, a Generation-Y career expert and author of one of my favorite books, *Getting From College to Career: 90 Things to Do Before You Join the Real World*, leads a range of terrific webinars in conjunction with The National Association of Colleges and Employers for college students new to LinkedIn (http://www. CareerServices.LinkedIn.com/webinar/).

8. **Ask and answer questions.** Ensure that you are getting and offering value by using this feature at the top of the page. You will be able to see current trends, curiosities, and concerns and, if answering a question, be able to prove you are a competent member of your industry.

9. **Use applications sparingly.** Whoever has the most applications DOES NOT win. Keep your profile easy on the eyes, professional looking, and focused on your unique benefits. Add applications only if they help you meet these three goals.

10. **See your LinkedIn profile as a work-in-progress.** Continue to sculpt your profile, invite new contacts, ask and answer questions, etc. The site only works if you are using it to reach out, connect with, and continue to build and engage in relationships.

Make sure that you connect with me and introduce yourself. Join my *Catalyst for Action* LinkedIn group to stay in-the-know on all things CAREERpreneurship.

SUCCESSwork: My LinkedIn Profile

Directions: Whether you are new or are returning to this network, follow the recommendations we just covered. To focus your work, answer the following questions:

What are your goals for using this online networking site?

_____

_____

_____

Who do you have to connect with to make this happen?

_____

_____

_____

What timeline are you setting for yourself to launch your profile?

_____

_____

_____

What kind of a commitment will you make to continue to build and strengthen your use of this network?

_____

_____

_____

Questions for Reflection

How is your use of this site allowing you to move towards your professional goals?

For you to double the impact of your networking, what would need to happen?

Twitter

Twitter (http://www.Twitter.com) is a microblogging site that allows you to, in mere seconds, set up a basic profile, send short messages or *tweets* (140 characters or less), and follow others' *tweets* (Note: Unlike most other online networking sites, you make the choice to *follow* people, and they make the choice to *follow* you. One person following another doesn't automatically mutually connect you). You also can send direct messages to anyone who is *following* you and easily monitor conversations others are having about you and your topics of concern.

The Top 10 Ways to Maximize Twitter

1. **Use your own name.** I wish I had done this when I set up my account. It allows people to find and *follow* you quickly and like LinkedIn, Twitter appears high up in search engines.

2. **Put your Unique Benefits Statement into your bio.** This will alleviate the need to figure out what to write in 160 characters and give you another opportunity to brand yourself consistently.

3. **Use your LinkedIn photo and a professional background.** You are using the same photo for consistency and professionalism. Twitter gives you several FREE backgrounds for your profile. Once you have gotten comfortable with Twitter, used it frequently, and have amassed some *followers*, consider investing in a customized background that enables your professional brand to pop. There are a lot of designers. Simply put "Twitter backgrounds" into a search engine to find them, see their samples, and get some quotes.

4. **Retweet.** At the end of each person's message that appears on your home page in the order that it was posted, you have the option to *Retweet (RT)*. This means that you are choosing to re-send it to everyone who is *following* you. This allows you to

share the value that others are providing AND shows the person or organization in the initial *tweet* that you found the message valuable.

5. *Follow* **job hunting, career, and business experts.** This allows you to get up to the minute news on prospective jobs, tips for your own hunt, and information on related career issues. Some of the experts featured in this book include:

alevit	heathbrothers
amandapearly	heatherhuhman
aubreylynch	keppie_careers
christinehassler	lindseypollak
danschawbel	lyjnow
downtownwoman	mwbuckingham
gabbybernstein	patriciajfoster
geninsight	roxanneravenel
genwecoach (Me!)	taigoodwin
greencareertracks	thewrightshui4u
gretchenrubin	vickisalemi

You can connect with these people and organizations simply by putting the name above after http://www.Twitter.com/ (e.g., http://www.Twitter.com/GenWeCoach).

6. *Follow* **anyone on your All-Star Team as well as prospective employers and other thought leaders and experts in your field.**

    To best engage these folks, consider *RTing* them and, mention their ideas specifically in your *tweets* by putting @ and then their *Twitter* name. For example, "On Chapter 10 of *Awaken Your CAREERpreneur* w/ @genwecoach. I recommend it!"

    I have had the best luck in searching for new people to *follow* by putting their names into a search engine followed by Twitter (e.g., Alexia Vernon Twitter).

    Also, once you have a critical mass of *followers*, you can *tweet* that you are looking for a particular opportunity and see if you get any bites from your *followers* (e.g., Seeking moms who are looking to start homebased biz for new webinar or

Looking for a PT sales job with green technology company in Bay Area). If you do this, however, make sure that you don't mind your current clients or employer seeing it and that you do it sparingly so as not to come off as needy or without your desired work for a prolonged period of time.

7. **DO NOT HAVE AN AUTORESPONDER.** If you want to reply to people who *follow* you to thank them or introduce yourself, that is glorious. Put @ _____ (their Twitter name) into your *tweet* box if you want everyone who *follows* you to read the message (e.g., @genwecoach: Excited to connect with you! On Chapter 10 of your book). If you want the message to be private, send a *direct message*. Whatever you do, make it personal or just don't do it at all. Nobody appreciates receiving stock correspondence, be it in an email inbox or on a social networking site.

8. **If searching for a job, go to TwitterJobSearch (http://www.TwitterJobSearch. com) and enter your desired job and location.** You can see who has *tweeted* about opportunities and *subscribe* so that new corresponding *tweets* are sent to you via Google. If you sign in with your Twitter account, you can save jobs to your account and add your resume to the site.

9. Use *hashtags*. *Hashtags* are a way to indicate that your *tweet* is related to a particular content area. This enables people to search and group *tweets* according to their interests. You create a *hashtag* simply by writing "#" followed by the word or phrase. For example, if you want to post about the book, you can use the *hashtag* **#CAREERpreneur** in your *tweet* (e.g., I'm doing some SUCCESSwork for #CAREERpreneur. Anyone else on Chapter 10?). I encourage you to set up a group on your Twitter account for **#CAREERpreneur** so that you can connect with other folks reading the book. You can do this by putting "**CAREERpreneur**" in your search box on your home page, save the search, and then click on it whenever you want to see if anyone has used the *hashtag*.

10. **Diane Danielson, the Founder of the Downtown Women's Clubs, has a 30-30-30-10 Rule. Follow it!** In order to increase the amount of people who *follow* and continue

to stay engaged with you, spend approximately 30% of your time promoting yourself, (e.g., New blog post: Check it out!), 30% of your time promoting others (e.g., @lyjnow is offering a fantastic new class for job seekers), 30% of your time just sharing information (e.g., @cnn reveals unemployment numbers going down), and the final 10% of your time revealing personal and appropriate items (e.g., I'm so excited for the first day of summer!). For this last category, consider asking a question that your *followers* can respond to. I can't tell you how many relationships I've started from asking a cooking question!

SUCCESSwork: My Twitter Profile

Directions: Whether you are new or are returning to this network, follow the recommendations we just covered. To focus your work, answer the following questions:

What are your goals for using this online networking site?

_____

_____

_____

_____

_____

Who do you have to connect with to make this happen?

_____

_____

_____

_____

What timeline are you setting for yourself to launch your profile?

_____

_____

_____

_____

What kind of a commitment will you make to continue to build and strengthen your use of this network?

_____

_____

_____

_____

Questions for Reflection

How is your use of this site allowing you to move towards your professional goals?

For you to double the impact of your networking, what would need to happen?

Facebook

Given that Facebook (http://www.Facebook.com) has more users than there are people in the United States, I'm not going to spend a lot of time telling you how to use the site, because chances are you are already on it. Facebook was designed to be a social network, and while you can certainly use it to reach out to *friends* for introductions, announce exciting professional news, or ask for career advice, you should feel free to use it primarily to connect with and keep in touch with friends and family. However, it's important to make sure that nothing you or your friends or family do compromises professional opportunities. Almost all companies and clients now search a person's online networking footprint, and Facebook is the most likely place they will start. Therefore, I'm going to offer you the following:

The Top 5 Ways to Ensure a Clean Facebook Footprint

1. **Utilize your privacy settings.** Make sure that only you and designated friends or groups are allowed to post to your *wall* and *tag* you in photos or videos. If anyone leaves anything on your page that does not magnify the brand you are trying to create, take it off immediately. Facebook owns the rights to this information and holds records of everything that is said by and about you. Facebook also has a tendency to update its privacy settings every few months, so you will want to continue to ensure that the information you want to have private stays private.

2. **Speak professionally in your public and less-public (remember, no message is really private) conversations.** In addition to following what I call the Grandma Rule (ensuring that everything you reveal about yourself is something you would want your grandma to know or see), watch grammar, expressing religious or political views, or speaking negatively about anyone or anything. I have too many horror stories of former students and clients who have lost opportunities not only because they revealed elicit behavior via their pictures and comments, but also for appearing sloppy or for holding opinions not in line with a company's or individual's culture or beliefs system.

3.   **Do not accept *friend requests* from anyone you don't know.** Not only can this predispose you to having your account hacked into it, but again, it connects you to people whose brands may contradict your own. (If we don't know each other, make sure you connect on *Alexia Vernon's Catalyst for Action* Facebook group and introduce yourself before requesting to become a *friend*.)

4.   **Limit the number of applications attached to your profile.** These applications can show up on search engines, cheapen the look of your account, and when sent to *friends*, be seen as spam.

5.   **Tell the truth.** I highly recommend limiting the personal information you reveal, and most importantly, DO NOT list your birth year. Make sure that anything you are choosing to add, be it your current or previous work history, hobbies, or cultural interests, are honest. There is nothing more embarrassing than a prospect bringing up a musical group you purport to love only to discover you don't know their newest hit (This happened to a client, and it made what should have been a stellar interview go south very quickly).

SUCCESSwork: Your Facebook Profile

Directions: Whether you are new or are returning to this network, follow the recommendations we just covered. To focus your work, answer the following questions:

What are your goals for using this online networking site?

_____

_____

_____

_____

Who do you have to connect with to make this happen?

_____

_____

_____

_____

What timeline are you setting for yourself to launch your profile?

_____

_____

_____

_____

What kind of a commitment will you make to continue to build and strengthen your use of this network?

_____

_____

_____

_____

Questions for Reflection

How is your use of this site allowing you to move towards your professional goals?

For you to double the impact of your networking, what would need to happen?

As you tinker with online networking as an ongoing CAREERpreneurship strategy, remember that it is one tool among many. While fear or inexperience is no reason to keep you away from LinkedIn, Twitter, or Facebook, be kind to yourself if you find any of the sites confusing, perhaps only moderately useful, or even boring. Dedicate some time to getting comfortable with them and then focus your efforts where you are feeling like you are getting the maximum bang for your buck.

Know that people really do get jobs, business, and other professional opportunities this way if at any point you are feeling discouraged or questioning your use of time. Here are six CAREERpreneurs who secured positions and business clients from their online networking to inspire you to diversify your mediums for relationship building and success engineering.

I found my job as a result of my profile on LinkedIn. I was not looking, and was gainfully employed with a Fortune 500 company, but an executive recruiter found me and started to entice me with <u>very attractive</u> job responsibilities and a <u>very attractive</u> financial offer. It took three months of her continuously calling before I caved in and commenced with the interview process and executive psychological examination. Three months later, I began the new gig. I've been with Cooper Power Systems since April 28, 2008 and have never looked back. (Stephen B. Weinstein, Manager of Marketing Communications at Cooper Power Systems, Pewaukee, WI)

This past year, my company HR Acuity has obtained two new customers for our on-demand solution exclusively using relationships developed on LinkedIn. Through groups I joined on the site, I connected and built relationships with two senior HR leaders who subsequently asked for more information on our product and signed on. The nice part about both of these relationships is that these leaders have continued to speak out to their colleagues about our product, and this has generated even more leads for our company! (Deborah Muller, President of HR Acuity, Chatham, NJ)

In the spring of 2009, I found myself unemployed through no choice of my own. I began going to what networking events I could, but many cost money and when you're unemployed that isn't necessarily the best option. I turned my focus to social media—predominantly Twitter and LinkedIn. After a bit of networking I was messaged by a company that was hiring. I had a lunch meeting with the CEO then 3 rounds of interviews and here I am working in the exact position I found through Twitter! One of the compliments I received was how well I branded myself online; it was a double win for me professionally. (Kelley R. Walker, Chief Interwebs Troublemaker at Guffly: Good Stuff for Good Living, Detroit, MI)

In January of 2008, I learned that my former company was going through some restructuring and that I was going to possibly be forced to relocate. Since my wife was pregnant, I have a young son and my whole family is here in Minnesota, I decided that I needed to start looking for a job. I felt selfish because I knew the economy sucked and that it wouldn't be easy, but I didn't want to move. I started my search online. Using LinkedIn.com, I found a company that I was interested in, and in March I reached out to them to see if they had anything available. They quickly shot back and said they did not but that we should stay in touch. Two-months later, they got back to me and asked me to meet! Four weeks later, they offered me a job! (Ryan May, Vice President at Risdall McKinney Public Relations, New Brighton, MN)

I reached out to my LinkedIn network in 2007 looking for someone who knew a decision maker at Williams Sonoma (WS). It turns out that one of my LinkedIn contacts went to business school with a guy who was a senior buyer at the company. She made an e-introduction; I sent my materials for my wood-fired grills (for the backyard and professional epicurean); and after a few months of negotiation and paperwork, we became a WS vendor. I never once met any of my WS people face-to-face during the process, and now we've been with them for 3 years!" (Benjamin Eisendrath, Owner of Grillworks, Inc., Washington, DC)

When I was a junior in a college in Pennsylvania, I attended a Public Relations conference. They suggested we all become members of MyRagan.com. It's like a Facebook but for communication professionals. I wasn't sure what it was all about, but I figured I'd play around with the site anyway. I listed in my profile that I was looking for a PR internship in New York City. After networking with a few other members of the site, I began talking to a CEO. He said he would gladly look at my resume and give me tips for getting an internship. Turns out he liked my resume enough to give me an internship with his company. When the internship was completed, he allowed me to freelance for the company while I finished up my college career. Once my college career was over, I moved to NYC and now I work with them full-time. (Lauren Hovey, Junior Account Executive/Junior Media Strategist at Ericho Communications, New York, NY)

Chapter Eleven

Resumes and Cover Letters CAREERpreneur Style

Whether or not you anticipate applying for a j-o-b in this or a future chapter of your CAREERpreneurship journey, you want to have an updated resume and cover letter at the ready. You just never know when you may be courted for a position that enables you to align perfectly your values, strengths, resources, and enthusiasms. I've even needed to submit my resume for certain contracts and grants as a business owner and consultant. CAREERpreneurs know that while they are working towards particular goals, they allow themselves to stay open and ready for possibilities that previously weren't even blips on their radar. And while resumes and cover letters are typically the most familiar pieces of professional promotional material, they are nevertheless very often misunderstood and therefore not created to get CAREERpreneurs the results they seek.

Just like your UBS, the purpose of your resume and cover letter is to show its recipients (who I will refer to as employers throughout the rest of the chapter for simplicity sake even though we know the recipients could be someone else, e.g., funders, prospective clients, etc.) how you can solve a problem or fill a need that is important to them. Yes, you are making a case for how fabulous you are, but only as your *fabulousness* makes you the best person to produce the results the employer is looking for! Everything you write in either document should be building a compelling story and providing evidence for how you do this.

The Employer-Centered Resume

There are two forms of resumes that allow you to show how you are uniquely poised to provide employers what they are looking for, the **chronological resume** (which lists all of your professional experiences from most current to most dated) and the **functional resume** (which lists the skills you have developed and your areas of expertise, irrespective of position). While I think functional resumes help Human Resources get to the qualifications of a candidate much more quickly than a chronological resume, the unfortunate truth is that most prefer the chronological one and online application systems will require it. Therefore, that's what we are going to look at.

The information in your chronological resume should be listed as follows:

1. **Contact information** (Name, Address, Phone Number, Email Address (Should be your name), and Website/Blog (ONLY if career-related))
2. **Objective** (This is phrased in the infinitive- To _____) and you adapt your UBS to meet the specific need(s) the employer you are applying to is looking to fill. You will customize this for each opportunity.)
3. **Summary** (This should list the 4-6 most impressive and relevant experiences, skills, or awards you have garnered.)
4. **Professional Experience** (Title of Company, Location (only if relevant and you have worked in many different regions), Job Title, and a **brief** results-oriented description of your role (use active verbs to state each responsibility); **Leave out** positions that are not relevant to the current one you are applying for, noting that some companies may insist you list everything or explain any gaps in employment in which case you will.)
5. **Education** (Year of Graduation or Years of Attendance, Name of School, Degree(s), and Focus of Study; include relevant certificates and continuing education)
6. **Miscellaneous** (Depending on what you most want to highlight—Professional Affiliations/Awards, or Special Skills—create and title this final category.)

7. **References** (**You don't need to mention them.** By applying for the position you are implying you have them. Don't waste precious space listing them or saying they are available upon request.)

Your resume should be no more than 1 page for every 4-5 positions you have held. Do whatever it takes, usually leaving off your earliest entry-level employment, to keep your resume under 3 pages even if you are a veteran in your field. Use a font and size that is professional and legible (usually Times New Roman, size 10-12). You and at least three sets of trusted eyes should proofread your resume to ensure that your grammar is correct, formatting is accurate and easy on the eyes, and that your WOW Factor jumps off the page.

Review the sample resume on the next page, and see how "Stephanie U. Chang" follows the recommendations we covered.

Stephanie U. Chang
1317 Via Correa Lane * Austin, TX 78727
Phone: (512) 333-0619 * stephanie@stephanieuchang.com

Objective: To empower companies through strategic curriculum design to embrace diversity as a core value for attracting and retaining employees, increasing productivity and results, and building a more cohesive and enjoyable workplace.

CAREER HIGHLIGHTS

5+ years as a Diversity Curriculum Designer, Employee Trainer, and Human Resources Generalist
Designed a New Hire Diversity Unit that increased employee retention by 20%
Employee-of-the-Month as a Trainer for the City of Henderson
Launched Award-Winning Newsletter for Austin Energy Initiative
Full-Tuition Scholarship to UNLV's Workforce Education and Development Graduate Program
St. Edward's University's Most Outstanding Graduate in the College of Liberal Arts

PROFESSIONAL EXEPRIENCE

August 2009- **Lake Travis Computer Systems**
August 2010 **Job Title: Training Curriculum Designer (Paid Internship)**
Description: Researched, developed, implemented, and evaluated written, web, and audio curriculum for 4-company training programs (New Hire, New Manager, Senior Leadership, and Sales Professional); Conceived, designed, and implemented Diversity Unit for New Hire program

October 2006- **City of Henderson**
May 2009 **Job Title: Employee Trainer**
Description: Taught a range of New Hire, Diversity, Customer Service, and Safety courses to impart knowledge, develop skills, and mold and solidify behavior; Developed, reviewed, and evaluated course materials; Met with affiliated programs to ensure training supported company goals, vision, and mission

August 2004- **Austin Energy Initiative (AEI)**
July 2006 **Job Title: HR Generalist**
Description: Liaised between employees and management in all employee-related issues; Oversaw payroll; Scheduled and maintained employee class attendance; Identified and made recommendations for efficiencies and new programs; Created and maintained multiple databases, including compliance; Maintained relationships with vendors; Started and edited company newsletter

September 2002- **St. Edwards University Department of Human Resources**
May 2004 **Job Title: Administrative Associate**
Description: Supported HR team in running all facets of department

EDUCATION

August 2006- **University of Nevada Las Vegas Department of Education**
August 2009 **Degree: MS in Workforce Education and Development (3.75 GPA)**

August 2000- **St. Edward's University**
May 2004 **Degree: BA in Sociology, Minor in Business (4.0 GPA)**

AWARDS AND AFFILIATIONS

National member of ASTD/**Vice President of Professional Development for ASTD Austin** * Full-tuition scholarship to UNLV * UNLV Workforce Education and Development Curriculum Committee * Most Outstanding Graduate from St. Edward's University's College of Liberal Arts * Active volunteer with Nevada Partnership for Homeless Youth and Greater Austin CARES

SUCCESSwork: *Dynamize* Your Resume

Directions: Look over your resume based on the preceding criteria and example. Before worrying about adding content, move existing information around so that it is first in the right format. That way you can read it the way your prospective employer will. (This is NOT the place to reinvent the wheel. Use your creativity within the required structure.) **Now, ask yourself, "*Who* is coming across on the page?" Does that person best represent the candidate that the employer MUST have to fill its need(s)?**

If your answer is anything but a resounding YES, go back to the job description. Create a detailed story of the candidate the company MUST HAVE NOW and customize the story *your* resume tells so that it is presenting the version of you the prospective employer most needs. This is not about creative fiction but rather narrative nonfiction. There are many truthful stories about our experiences we can tell. You are shaping the one that will be picked up, read, and appreciated by your prospective employer.

For example, our hypothetical applicant Stephanie U. Chang comes to a prospective employer with myriad experiences at the intersections of human resources and training. From her Objective, Career Highlights, and Lake Travis Computer Systems position, we know that Stephanie is focused on presenting herself as a rising leader in her field who is prepared for and focused on a curriculum design position centered on workplace diversity awareness. From the particular Highlights she lists and her Awards and Affiliations, a prospective employer also gets a sense of who Stephanie is as a person. She clearly has a commitment to serve in her community and has been recognized for outstanding achievement both in the classroom and in her previous positions. She has piloted several projects, such as a company newsletter and new curriculum, attesting to her ability both to launch new ventures and, when possible, link them to measurable results (her New Hire Diversity Unit increased employee retention by 20%). You will get to see how Stephanie builds on this narrative in her cover letter.

While the structure and bones of your resume will stay the same for each submission, **customize all sections for every application** (particularly your Objective,

Summary or Career Highlights, and Job Responsibilities) to show concretely your experience providing the kinds of solutions the specific employer seeks. If Stephanie decided she wanted to return to an HR Generalist position, she would need to adjust her Objective, Career Highlights, and how she talks about her most recent positions to make herself pop for a prospective employer.

Questions for Reflection

In 30-seconds (or 2-3 sentences), how would you share that you are hands-down the BEST person for the position you are applying for?

How can you use your answer to the above question to guide the development of your accompanying cover letter? (This will be discussed in the next session.)

If any hesitancy or fear surrounding the application pops up, how can you use the personal foundation tools and healthy habits in thinking, feeling, and behaving you have cultivated to diffuse them?

The Employer-Centered Cover Letter

Your cover letter is your opportunity to craft, in narrative form, the story you are hoping HR will put together from your resume. Unless you are explicitly told not to include one, or an online application process makes it impossible to attach, ALWAYS include a cover letter with your application.

Like a resume, a cover letter has a basic format:

1. **Your Contact Information** (Name, Address, Phone Number, Email Address (Should be your name), and Website/Blog (ONLY if career-related))
2. **Employer Contact Information and Salutation** (Include the full address, Name of the person you are applying to (Mr. or Ms. _____), and the Date. Begin your letter Mr. or Ms. _____ . If the name of the person you are applying to is not included, find it out!)
3. **Your Objective or UBS** (NEVER begin with "I am applying for…" You can include it towards the end of your first paragraph after a strong, favorable impression has been created. Begin with your name and go straight into what you will do for the employer).
4. **Why Should I Care About You?** (In the first paragraph, capture the reader's attention, establish credibility, and wet the appetite for what is to come. State why you are applying for this position. Emphasize years in the field, your range of experiences, and noteworthy education. If you have conducted an informational interview with the person you are applying to or someone else in the company, have been referred, etc., mention it early on.)
5. **Provide Evidence** (In paragraph form or in bullet points, list up to 5 reasons (e.g., skills, experiences, awards, etc.) that show how you have and will continue to achieve the necessary results. Make sure your brand or WOW Factor comes across).
6. **Bring It Back to the Company** (If you can, prove that you have done your due diligence and know about the company. And not just what it does, but also who

it employs, the culture it facilitates, and the kind of impact it has had in the local, national, or international community.)

7. **Wrap Up Powerfully** (Briefly and enthusiastically mention that you are looking forward to speaking further. Remind the reader that follow-up will continue to be about showing her or him how you will help the company in the way it needs.)

Because a cover letter is in narrative paragraph form, some of the parts mentioned above might overlap or go in a slightly different order. This is fine. Just make sure that no step is overlooked (or expanded upon too much).

   Michael DiMaggio, PHR, the Director of Human Resources at Fidelity Engineering Corporation in Washington, D.C. says, the Top 3 things he looks for are: *brevity, how a candidate's background matches his needs, and an applicant's preferred contact information.* On the flipside, he guarantees a cover letter (and its accompanying resume) is headed straight for the garbage when an applicant *includes a detailed work history covering everything in a resume, an assumption of selection (e.g., "I'll call you to schedule my interview"), or personal information not relevant to the position (e.g., "I have a spouse and three children.").*

Keep your cover letter to 1-full page.

Sign your letter if snail mailing it, and follow the same resume proofreading procedures to concretize a positive first impression.

Have a look at "Stephanie U. Chang's" cover letter. After reviewing it, ask yourself:

As a reader, what are the top three things you take away from the story Stephanie is creating about herself?

How has she taken the cover letter template and made it her own?

Stephanie U. Chang

1317 Via Correa Lane
Austin, TX 78727
Phone: (512) 333-0619
stephanie@stephanieuchang.com

Loehman and Fitzpatrick, Inc.
27 West Street
Austin, TX 78701
Attention: Ms. Lucia Rivera

September 15, 2010

Dear Ms. Rivera,

My name is Stephanie U. Chang and I empower companies through strategic curriculum development to embrace diversity as a core value for attracting and retaining employees, increasing productivity and results, and building a more cohesive and enjoyable workplace. With 5-years experience in the fields of employee training and human resources, I know I can take Loehman and Fitzpatrick, Inc. to the next level of success and community impact. Therefore, I am submitting my cover letter and resume for your full-time Diversity Curriculum Specialist position.

I learned about this opportunity from Thomas White, the Vice President of Membership at today's Austin ASTD luncheon, where I am the new Vice President of Professional Development. As a former Diversity Manager at Loehman and Fitzpatrick, Inc., Mr. White believes that my professional experience, education, and community involvement will make me successful in the role and a good fit with your company culture that prides itself on Inward Excellence, Outward Service.

I earned my BA in Sociology from St. Edward's University and just finished my M.S. in Workforce Education and Development from the University of Nevada Las Vegas (UNLV) where I graduated with a 3.75 GPA. In addition to 40-hours of graduate coursework in diversity and inclusion, adult learning, curriculum design, and training strategies, I worked part-time as a Trainer for the City of Henderson, volunteered 10 hours a week with Nevada Partnership for Homeless Youth, and I served on the curriculum committee of our department. I also recently completed an internship at Lake Travis Computer System's Office of Diversity here in Austin where I launched a new diversity unit for New Hires. **As a result of my program, the company has reported retaining 20% more employees!**

I look forward to discussing further the many innovative solutions I have developed in my career and, most importantly, how I can benefit Loehman and Fitzpatrick, Inc. as it moves into its 25th anniversary year and opens its first international office. Kindly contact me via email or phone.

Sincerely,
(signature)
Stephanie U. Chang

SUCCESSwork: The *Undismissable* Cover Letter

Directions: You guessed it! You are going to utilize the recommendations for cover letters, the sample cover letter above, and the directions in the previous resume SUCCESSwork as well as the follow-up Questions for Reflection to create your own employer-centered cover letter. Even if you are not applying for a specific position at this moment, signal to the world that you are ready for new opportunities by having all of your materials, including a dynamic cover letter, ready for submission.

Questions for Reflection
How does it feel to have your resume AND cover letter templates created?
What pops in these documents that you will want to highlight further in an interview via examples and stories?
What SUCCESSwork will you give yourself to ensure that the *you* in your application materials comes across in your informational interviewing, online networking, etc.?

Now that you have your templates for your resume and cover letter completed, go gangbusters on applying for those positions and opportunities that enable you to close the gap from your calling to your career!

When applying through an online channel, follow all of the steps the organization has outlined. Submit online, via email, or through snail mail as required. If submitting via email, paste your cover letter in the body of the email AND attach it along with your resume as Microsoft Word attachments. Aim not only to send your materials to the person listed in the call for employment, who is usually an HR representative and not an expert in your field. Use your detective skills as Stephen did in Chapter 9 to find out who the Hiring Manager or your future boss would be, and send the person your cover letter and resume as well. Follow-up with anyone you submit to via email or snail mail within 10 days and every 10-14 days after.

Resist the temptation to adjust your employment strategy to looking primarily for jobs online, in newspapers, or at local career fairs. This will expose you to less than a quarter of the opportunities out there. Continue putting relationships first via the methods we have discussed in previous chapters, such as establishing and building your connections through the development of an All-Star Team, informational interviewing, and networking face-to-face or through online media. Approach these opportunities with the faith that they will lead to application and ultimately employment opportunities, and keep tweaking your resume and cover letter so that you show each employer the candidate that is most uniquely poised to provide the solutions *they* are looking for!

Chapter Twelve

Rehearsing for Interview Success

N ow that you've created your resume and cover letter, potentially started applying for positions you were recommended for from your networking and informational interviewing, and have refined your vision board so that it reflects opportunities on the horizon, it's time to prepare for interviews. While the interview is a cornerstone of securing a job or consulting position, more and more individual purchasers and vendors are using them when deciding from whom to purchase a product or service. And interviewing really is like public speaking in that the more you rehearse, the more easily the skill will come. You will be able to show up to speak and not have to worry about remembering everything you want to cover. It will already be in your bones!

The 7 Categories of Interview Questions

One of the key differences between informational interviewing and traditional interviewing is that in theory you are in the role of interviewee in the latter. However, if you show up to a job interview—or an interview with a prospective client—with the mindset that you are still a key player in running the show and that you have as much to learn as she or he has to learn from you, your success will increase.

In order to prepare for interview success, you must learn the different categories of interview questions, identify questions you are likely to be asked, and prepare and rehearse your answers to them OUT LOUD.

1. **Introductory/Setting the Stage Questions**

   These are questions that an interviewer will ask at the very start to get a feel for your personality and diffuse nervousness. (e.g., *"How are you this morning?" "What about this weather we've been having?"*)

   Your aim is to be confident, personable, enthusiastic, and show reciprocity. Craft answers that reveal a little bit about who you are and establish yourself as an equal by asking appropriate questions in response. (e.g., *"I'm terrific, and how has your morning been?" "When the sun is shining, it's hard for me to be anything but dandy; are you a summer weather person or do you prefer a snowy day?"*)

2. **Verification Questions**

   These questions ask you to confirm the credentials and experience that you have listed on your resume, cover letter, LinkedIn profile, proposal, press materials, etc.

   A typical opening may be, *"Tell me about yourself,"* followed by questions asking you to talk through previous key roles and responsibilities. Make sure that you have memorized all of this information so that it is accurate, concise, and complete.

3. **Case/Scenario Questions**

   These problem-solving questions enable you to show how you find solutions when you are unsure of the answer. You can identify common difficult situations in your work that you are likely to be asked about and, just as importantly, get clear on how you analyze information and solve problems so that regardless of the case, you can show how you would approach it.

   Two samples questions in this category include, *"How would you get the answer to _____?"* or *"How do you get two supervisor's conflicting tasks accomplished?"*

4. **Self-Assessment Questions**

   These questions ask you to discuss your perceptions of yourself (or your product or service). They often require you to identify strengths and weaknesses. When talking about your strengths, you want to select the ones that will be most relevant for the position and company you are interviewing for. On the flipside, you want to identify a real weakness (or, as I recommend to CAREERpreneurs, explain that you see it as *an area for growth*). Refrain from empty answers like *"I'm a perfectionist"* that sound like you are evading an answer and, on the other side of the spectrum, identifying weaknesses that are major liabilities (e.g., *"I have a hard time meeting deadlines."* or *"I'm chronically late for appointments."*). Doing some self-assessment and making a list of all of your areas for growth will enable you to narrow your answers down to three appropriate answers (e.g., *"I have a hard time self-advocating in the face of conflict."*) and take action in strengthening any important skill or behavioral deficits.

5. **Behavioral Questions**

These questions, typically hypothetical scenarios, are designed to show an employer how you are likely to respond and take action in the workplace. They frequently have a clear "right" answer, such as the question, *"If you knew that a colleague were doing something unethical, how would you handle it?"* Trust me, the only answer the person asking such a question wants to hear is, *"I'd report it to my direct supervisor immediately."*

Another generic behavioral question you may be asked is *"Can you give me a specific example of how you did that?"* in response to something you say you have done in the past. This question is often asked as a follow-up to questions about strengths and weaknesses, so make sure you have those stories ready. *"How do you respond to conflict in the workplace?"* is another popular question in this category since being human is about moving through obstacles.

6. **Style Questions**

In these types of questions you will be asked to identify the way you work best in a variety of categories. *"How would you describe your leadership style?"* *"What way do you communicate best with others?"* *"How can others best communicate with you?"* *"What enables you to operate at peak performance?"*

If you have ever completed a DISC or an MBTI, the most common workplace behavioral and personality assessments, make sure you remember and can discuss those results. While some employers will be screening for someone who fits a particular profile, most will be interested in finding employees who are clear on what catalyzes their success. Even if the person conducting the interview wants a particular answer, being transparent will protect you and the company (e.g., If you are someone who is Introverted, Intuitive, Feeling, and Perceiving, you really don't want a position that requires you to be Extroverted, Sensing, Thinking, and Judging). It would be a set-up to fail.

7.   **Zany Questions**

These questions can be used for a couple of purposes, such as to lighten the mood or to test your ability to think on your feet. What's important is not composing the world's most original answer. Rather, success will be assessed by your ability to come up with something while maintaining your confidence and owning it.

Examples in this category that my clients and I have been asked include, *"If you had to be an animal, what kind of animal would you be and why?" "What city in the world best represents your personality?" "If you had to do one professional task the rest of your life, what would it be?"*

SUCCESSwork: What are *Your* Questions?

Directions: For each of the categories of interview questions, identify 5-7 questions you believe you will be asked. In guesstimating your questions, make sure you are considering the vision, mission, and values of the company, the culture of your field, and the chief responsibilities and daily tasks of the position.

Introductory/Setting the Stage Questions

1. _____

2. _____

3. _____

4. _____

5. _____

6. _____

7. _____

Verification Questions

1. _____

2. _____

3. _____

4. _____

5. _____

6. _____

7. _____

Case/Scenario Questions

1. _____

2. _____

3. _____

4. _____

5. _____

6. _____

7. _____

Self-Assessment Questions

1. _____

2. _____

3. _____

4. _____

5. _____

6. _____

7. _____

Behavioral Questions

1. _____

2. _____

3. _____

4. _____

5. _____

6. _____

7. _____

Style Questions

1. _____

2. _____

3. _____

4. _____

5. _____

6. _____

7. _____

Zany Questions

1. _____

2. _____

3. _____

4. _____

5. _____

6. _____

7. _____

Questions for Reflection

Based on the questions you have identified, how prepared do you currently feel for a potential interview?

What work in self, skill, and behavioral development will be necessary for you to interview at the top of your game?

Refrain from answering your questions . . . for now.

Top 20 Interview DOs

Patty Foster, a Senior Corporate Recruiter, says that she, and the companies she works for, screen for employees who demonstrate an *"I can' attitude, the ability to think critically and be resourceful, and a willingness to go the extra mile without expecting an immediate reward."*

Regardless of the questions that you are asked, there are a series of considerations and action steps you can take to ensure that *who* you show up as best reflects *you* and gives the interviewer(s) what they are looking for in their ideal candidate.

1. **Know the name and title of anyone who will be interviewing you and the purpose of the interview.** Is it a group interview? Will you just be doing a 5-minute credential screening with HR? Are you meeting with the senior executive team? (Unlikely, by the way, for a first interview.) Make sure you are walking into a situation you can visualize clearly and prepare for accordingly.

2. **Identify your WOW Factor or the 3 things that set you apart that you want your interviewer to hold onto after the interview.** Make sure that they are *sticky*! One of them should be the results you have delivered and solutions you have come up with that would matter to this company. Another should be something significant about *who* you are (e.g., a champion hockey player or avid hiker). The third is up to you and is usually a story *(refer back to your SUCCESSwork from Chapter 5)* that shows you in action.

3. **Continue to work on your Personal Foundation so that you are staying calm, confident, balanced, and engaged in learning and growth.** This will come through in your communication in and outside of the interview.

4. **Get a good night's sleep the night before so that you show up looking and behaving energetically.** Stop any preparation at least two hours before you go to bed so that you can have a deep, relaxed sleep.

5. **Eat a meal approximately 1-2 hours before your interview.** You want to have energy without being in the throes of digestion or needing to use the bathroom.

6. **Practice your answers out loud the day of your interview.** While you don't want to obsess over them, do give yourself that final dress rehearsal.

7. **Dress appropriately.** As a rule, men want to wear a suit and tie and women want to wear a professional looking dress or a skirt or pants suit. Have just one item that pops. This is typically a tie or shirt for men and an accessory for women (e.g., earrings, necklace, ring, bracelet, or shoes. No open toes or high pumps!). If the company has an ultra-relaxed dress environment, jeans or sweats, dress just one step up. This means slacks/skirt and a dress shirt. If the office dress culture is business casual or dressier, which most are, bring out the more professional duds.

8. **Arrive JUST 10-15 minutes before your scheduled interview time.** You want to be early without being a burden on interviewers or their staff.

9. **Bring 3 copies of your resume and your cover letter.** While most interviewers will tell you who will be in the room, be ready for unexpected folks by having a copy of your materials prepared for each of them.

10. **Shake hands firmly and appropriately (watch squeezing too hard that you make the other person uncomfortable) with each person you meet.**

11. **Make eye contact immediately with your interviewer, sustain it, and watch the tendency to let eye contact evolve into staring.**

12. **Use humor as appropriate.** Remember, interviewers are most likely going to work with you and, whether they admit it or not, are considering whether they want to spend a minimum of 1/3 of their life with you.

13. **Make a personal connection with the interviewer.** No matter the length of the interview, (often times a first one may be no more than 15 minutes), aim to communicate *who* you are and not simply *what* you do. Create a lasting narrative about yourself centered on your brand. And smile as you talk!

14. **Answer questions clearly and concisely.** Know your main points for each and hit them. Be truthful in what you say and ensure that you are answering exactly what is asked.

15. **Focus on the 3 top things you want to leave your interviewee remembering.** Answer and ask questions to meet your goals.

16. **Ask questions that could not have been answered by you doing research.**

> *"Remember that the questions [you] ask of a prospective employer are just as important as the questions [you] are asked. Not gathering enough information about the company, the position, and what's expected to be successful is like buying a house without doing a proper inspection. A truly successful interview means both sides have the information they need to make a good decision."* (Tai Goodwin, The Career Makeover Coach)

Think about using what you have learned to formulate your questions (e.g., *"I have been following the development of your satellite office in Issaquah, WA. Do you envision that it will offer the same services as the Las Vegas office or have a specific community focus?" "How is the company responding to the expansion of (insert name of competitor)?"*). Asking questions shows that you are genuinely interested in working for a company and that you are as determined to find the right professional fit as you are to receive a steady paycheck.

17. **Ask appropriate and informative questions about your interviewers.** Ask why they came to work for the company, what they enjoy most about their roles, or how they know when they have found an employee who is a good fit for the company. People LOVE to talk about themselves! Most importantly, learn interviewer's preferred communication medium (e.g., email, office phone, LinkedIn, etc.). This will show that you want to communicate the way other people can hear you and enable you to follow-up with you interviewers appropriately.

18. **Find out the timeline for the selection process.** Will your interviewer or a member of HR be in touch? When? By the end of the week? In 1-2 months? 6 months from now? Also, learn what the next steps are. Most companies will have at least another interview with more members of the department, either in person or on the phone.

19. **Ask for a business card from each interviewer.** Follow-up with a 2-3 sentence email or handwritten card within 24-hours using the following template.

> Dear <u>First Name or Mr. or Ms. Last Name</u>,
>
> Because of my (stick in your UBS), I'm confident that I am the right person to (fill in the overarching job responsibility). (Add a personalized sentence or two reflecting what came up in the interview.)
>
> Thank you so much for meeting with me today to discuss (title of position). I look forward to the opportunity to bring my experiences and enthusiasm in (your field or fields) to (name of company).
>
> Regards,
> Your Full Name

20. **Do follow-up as appropriate.** You asked what the timeline is so you want to do what makes sense. If this was just a quarterly screening of new talent, follow-up every 2-3 months. If this is a position that is to be filled within the next 1-2 months (which is typical), follow-up every 10-14 days. Because you asked your interviewers' preferred method of communication, use it.

What if My Interview is on the Phone?

Many companies are now conducting an initial round of interviews on the phone, particularly if they are considering you or other candidates from outside the area. While you will want to follow all of the preparation and performance steps we just covered, you also want to consider the following. **First**, make sure that you are in a quiet space and on a phone line with a secure signal (ideally a land line). **Second**, keep in mind that the person or people on the other side of the phone will only have your voice from which to paint a picture of you from. Therefore, you will want to ensure that your energy and enthusiasm are even higher than they would be in a traditional face-to-face interview. Listen keenly so that you answer exactly what is being asked of you without interrupting the other person or people speaking. **Third**, dressing in your professional duds will help you keep a more formal tone in conversation. **Fourth**, you have the opportunity to have some notes in front of you. Seize it! I recommend your resume, so that you are sure to be accurate with any of those verification questions. Also, keep handy the top three pieces of information you want to impart, any questions that you know you want to ask, and something to take notes with. **Finally**, public speakers stand when working a room for a reason. I encourage you to conduct the interview up on your feet to move freely as you speak. Doing so will get energy flowing throughout your body, help you speak clearly and loudly, diffuse fear, and enhance the expressiveness of your voice.

SUCCESSwork: Preparing Your Interview Answers (A 3-Step Process)

Directions: 1ˢᵗ Step- Before you compose your answers to the interview questions you have identified, reflect on *who* you want to show up as and *what* you will want to communicate by the end of the interview (your WOW Factor). Narrow your aspirations down to 3 overarching goals.

e.g., I want to prove my UBS. (I solve fiscal shortfalls for Health Maintenance Organizations (HMOs).)

e.g., I want to communicate my brand. (Collaborative, Intuitive, and Energetic)

e.g., I want to have my interviewer remember that I make a mean peanut-butter chocolate-chip cookie!

Go back through previous SUCCESSwork, particularly from Chapters 3, 5, 7, and 11, so that you are drawing from the *smart* work you have already created.

Goal 1:

_____

_____

_____

Goal 2:

_____

_____

_____

Goal 3:

_____

_____

_____

2nd Step- For each of your goals, identify *how* you will do this in your interview.

e.g., For proving UBS: I will share 3 concrete examples of how I have done this.

e.g., For communicating brand: I will mention how I've used the strengths of previous work groups to increase results, ask my interviewer what enables her to trust her team, and smile while speaking.

e.g., For sharing my cookie prowess: I will find a place to insert that I'm a favorite at company parties because of my kickin' peanut-butter chocolate-chip cookie recipe.

Goal 1 Strategy:

_____

_____

_____

Goal 2 Strategy:

_____

_____

_____

Goal 3 Strategy:

_____

_____

_____

3rd Step- Finally, compose answers to the questions you created, ensuring that they encompass the information you gathered in Steps 1 and 2.

Because you will be speaking your answers, craft them by saying them orally. Once you have settled on content and wording that you like, write them down for continued rehearsal.

Interview Answers

Introductory/Setting the Stage

1. _____

2. _____

3. _____

4. _____

5. _____

6. _____

7. _____

Verification

1. _____

2. _____

3. _____

4. _____

5. _____

6. _____

7. _____

Case/Scenario

1. _____

2. _____

3. _____

4. _____

5. _____

6. _____

7. _____

Self-Assessment

1. _____

2. _____

3. _____

4. _____

5. _____

6. _____

7. _____

Behavioral

1. _____

2. _____

3. _____

4. _____

5. _____

6. _____

7. _____

Style

1. _____

2. _____

3. _____

4. _____

5. _____

6. _____

7. _____

Zany

1. _____

2. _____

3. _____

4. _____

5. _____

6. _____

7. _____

Aim to practice the answers OUT LOUD a minimum of an hour each day for AT LEAST a week before your first interview and throughout your interviewing process. This will ensure that they stay polished, and you can recall the range of material you want to share. Also, this will prepare you to adjust your answers to the questions you actually get asked in a way that reflects everything you seek to achieve and still enables you to sound natural.

Questions for Reflection
How is your interview performance evolving through your rehearsals?

What is the relationship between your confidence and the power of your interview responses?

After you interview, give yourself enough time to digest but not so long you forget what transpired (approximately 2-3 hours), and ask: *In future interviews, what do you want to do more of? What do you want to do less of? What should you keep exactly as is?*

Your interview success really is in your hands. If you want to show up at 100%, you need to rehearse at 100%. Get out of your head and on your feet as quickly as possible to practice so that your ideas, word choice, body language, and sense of self make you irresistibly attractive to your prospective employers. Consider filming yourself early on so that you can see how you appear for others, and adjust anything that doesn't reflect the messages you want someone to walk away with. And most importantly, visualize yourself interviewing successfully and diffuse fear with your mantras, deep breathing, and exercise so that what you are putting out into the universe is setting you up for the achievement that you deserve.

SUCCESSwork: Phase 3 Mid-Point Reflection

Directions: As you have done in previous chapters, bring yourself back to that physical environment where whole body reflection can take place. Make sure that the following questions and your answers to previous SUCCESSwork are in tow. Take some time to release any tension you might be holding in your body. Bring your awareness to your breath, and take some nice, deep inhalations and exhalations. Once you have had

some delicious moments of relaxation, muse on the following questions. Record your answers so that you can continue to track and celebrate your progress!

1. What have you learned in the first half of *The CAREERpreneur's Essential Tools* section that has been of most value?

    _____

    _____

    _____

2. What has been the impact of adopting a CAREERpreneur's mindset over the last 4 chapters on yourself and those in your professional and personal life?

    _____

    _____

    _____

3. Where is there additional room for learning and growth?

    _____

    _____

    _____

4. What SUCCESSwork are you giving yourself around personal foundation, building a network, and using CAREERpreneurship tools to increase your capacity for success?

    _____

    _____

    _____

5. How has your professional vision of *who* you want to be, *what* you want to be doing, and *how* you will be showing up to opportunities evolved?

    _____

    _____

    _____

6. What will be the payoff for giving your all to the remainder of the *Awaken Your CAREERpreneur* process?

    _____

    _____

    _____

Chapter Thirteen

I Survived Round One, Now What?

This chapter's SUCCESSwork should be completed when you have actually gone out and interviewed for a position or business opportunity. If you are not there quite yet, still continue reading (so you know what SUCCESSwork lies ahead!) and then spend some time ensuring that the SUCCESSwork you devised for yourself in previous chapters has gotten translated into action.

Perhaps it's time to check-in with your personal foundation work. See if there are any new or reoccurring limiting beliefs that need to be *recycled.* I'd be lying if I said that there wasn't at least a time or two each month where I fell back into comparing myself to old friends or colleagues and, as a result, lamented what I have yet to achieve rather than celebrated how far I've come. And I've been on my CAREERpreneurship journey for quite a while now. I know, however, that each time I fall back into an old habit—whether it's this one or any other—that it's an opportunity to notice the choice I'm making, stop it, and recommit to a more nourishing one.

You may decide that you want to dedicate some more time to online networking. The more relationships you start and build, the more possibilities you have for informational interviews and All-Star Team members. And maybe you even want to connect with other CAREERpreneurs. Therefore, you are going to play on Twitter with the *hashtag* #CAREERpreneur and see who else is going on this journey, compare insights, and hold one another accountable for completing your SUCCESSwork.

Remember that wherever you are is exactly where you need to be! As we move more and more into developing skills and materials that are pivotal to CAREERpreneurship, ensure that you are still creating healthy, success-inducing habits in thinking, feeling, and behaving. A mindset and worldview rooted in possibility and gratitude will have the greatest impact on catalyzing and sustaining your career success and overall life satisfaction.

Now, if you have gone out and interviewed, regardless of how well you feel you did, I sure hope that you did the follow-up SUCCESSwork from the last chapter and engaged in some critical reflection. Then, I hope you treated yourself to a nice meal out or a movie. (Or as I have always done in penny-pinching times, hung out in a local park with some juicy chic lit.) While you will continue to follow-up with your interviewers as appropriate based on the timeline for hiring (or embarking on a business relationship), you want to be ready for the next steps in the process should you continue to be a candidate: the follow-up interview (or interviews), the offer, and if applying for a j-o-b, the lead up to your first day.

The Follow-Up Interview

If you are applying for anything beyond an entry-level job or an internship, you will likely go through one to two more rounds of interviews. According to Quintessential Careers, the chances of you getting your position at this point are between 25%-50%. You're in good shape; however, you still are not yet at the homestretch. If you continue to be a candidate for the position, you will most likely be notified within 2-3 weeks of your interview. If the timeline for hiring passes and you do not receive a notification from the company, take a deep breath and bulldoze forward. *What did you learn? How did you grow? What smart action can you take next?*

Until you are sure you will *not* get called for another interview, proceed as if you will and get ready. You have three chief goals in your forthcoming interviews:

1. **Show that you are a fit for the position.** (Yup, back to the ole: *How do you fill the need and provide solutions better than anyone else under consideration?* Also, how are

you a fit *in* the job and *with* the company? Connect with everyone you speak or meet with in follow-up interviews, even if there are many people interacting with you simultaneously. Maintaining eye contact is key. Also, use names to address people whenever possible, and direct responses and questions to all in attendance, not just the person who asked.)

2. **Show that your brand is consistent.** (Most companies want to see if the impression you cast during your first interview stays the same. Make sure that *who* you are comes across just like it did in the first interview. To this end, use language, wear clothing, and sculpt body language as you did the first time. It worked so resist the temptation to tinker too much!)

3. **Show that you have done some work between interviews and both want and deserve this opportunity.** (Expect to be pushed harder with each subsequent conversation and interview you go through. You will have more behavioral, case, and self-assessment questions. You will be asked for more examples to prove your statements. You may even be invited to take a personality, leadership, or communication style test or assessment. Because you want to co-run this show, make sure that you are even clearer and articulate about the results you can deliver in your new role. Demonstrate that you have thought through any company information you were given last time. Know what you could achieve in your first six months in the position and share it.)

SUCCESSwork: Refining the Interview Rehearsal Script

Directions: Fill in your answers to the following questions. This will ensure that you are continuing to prepare for interviews, deliver in them, and follow-up smartly.

1. Which of your anticipated questions were you asked? How do you want to respond to them if asked a similar question again?

_____

_____

_____

_____

2.   Which of your answers made the greatest impact? Why? How can you refine your answer so that it comes out differently and just as successfully next time?

_____

_____

_____

3.   Were there any unexpected questions that came up? (Whether you handled them effortlessly or struggled through them, make a note of this for subsequent interviews with this or another company or prospective client.)

_____

_____

_____

4.   What questions did you ask that you want to make sure NOT to ask again? (YOUR questions should not stay the same.)

_____

_____

_____

5.   Are there new questions that have emerged for you that you would like to ask? (Your answer should be YES!)

_____

_____

_____

_____

6. It is possible that in future interviews you will meet with anywhere from 2-5 additional interviewers (e.g., managers, senior managers, vice presidents, and colleagues) and that your interviews could happen on the phone, in the office, or over a meal. What do you need to do to feel comfortable in each of these contexts?

    _____

    _____

    _____

7. What do you want to know prior to the next interview? (e.g., Who will be in the room? Where does this mean I am in the process? What will the interviewers be looking to learn from the interview?) How will you ask for this information when someone calls to set the interview(s) up so that you are prepared?

    _____

    _____

    _____

Questions for Reflection

How well are you achieving your three follow-up goals in your rehearsals?

How are you rehearsing to ensure you create an enjoyable experience for your interviewers?

The Negotiation

Be prepared to discuss salary or fee by your second interview, if not before. Many positions are no longer posting salaries or salary ranges which makes answering the question, *"What are your salary requirements?"* a little tricky and possibly uncomfortable. To guard against this, learn the salary range for your position or fee for your product or service. Take into account **size of company** (e.g., number of employees), **sector** (e.g., nonprofit, corporate, small business, government), **industry** (e.g., engineering, education, finance, healthcare), and **location** (e.g., major city, smaller city, suburb, rural). **Indeed.com** is my favorite place to look for salary ranges (although it's usually based on less than a quarter of positions). **SimplyHired.com** also does a nice job filtering through different company contexts.

Once you come up with a range for yourself, (e.g., An administrative assistant in New York, NY working for a private university makes $35,000-$45,000), get clear on why you deserve the amount you are gunning for. (Ask for 5%-10% higher than you are expecting so that there is some wiggle room for negotiation.)

SUCCESSwork: Why You Are Worth the Higher End of the Salary Spectrum

Directions: Identify the 3-5 reasons you are worth what you are worth. Whatever the reasons, link them to the results you can deliver. (e.g., *"Having received my MBA at the HEC Paris makes me uniquely equipped not simply to "manage" European accounts but also to ensure that our clients are treated the way they want to be treated."*)

10 Attractive Experiences (As long as you create the bridge back to solutions!)

1. Many years in a field or role
2. Experience working with (on a paid or volunteer basis) a leader (e.g., company or person) in the field

3. Education or credentialing above the norm

4. A degree from a prestigious college or university

5. Experience working or living abroad

6. Fluency in more than 1 language

7. Industry awards

8. Publishing articles/books

9. Elected positions in related professional associations

10. You are an industry speaker/presenter/media commentator

Questions for Reflection

Which of your reasons will have the greatest impact on your prospect? (Begin and end with them, book ending your less compelling reason.)

What will enable you to speak your desired amount with confidence and commitment?

What is most important for you to accomplish in your negotiation? (e.g., making the ask, securing a certain amount, etc.) What are your needs, what are your desires, and what are you willing to concede?

This last group of question is important so that you know how to rehearse for and perform during the salary negotiation. (Remember, you are a co-host of this show.) If you simply want to have the audacity to ask for more money than makes you comfortable, great, ask for it. If you really want a particular amount, ensure that you are asking for closer to 10% higher than you expect to get. Knowing what you want, whatever it is, can give you a way to gauge success and organize your strategy.

5 Salary Negotiation DOs

1. **DO** frame obtaining the money you are worth as a creative and confidence-building activity.
2. **DO** rehearse your negotiation out loud!
3. **DO** let negotiation be a give and take. (Although you don't want the conversation to go on endlessly, it's okay to have it go back and forth a few times for each person to get what is desired.) **You never need to accept an opportunity or a salary/fee on the spot. Give yourself the time to mull it over.**
4. **DO** *Recycle-the-Box* when it comes to offering an employer ways to compensate for a lower-salary. Consider flex-time, extended vacation, an adjusted job description, or a learning stipend in exchange for a lower wage.
5. **DO** get any offer in writing. This protects you and your future employer or client.

5 Salary Negotiation Don'ts

1. **DON'T** bring up money. Aim to let your prospect mention it AND make the first offer. The only exception to this is if you believe the company or person will be offering significantly less than you want. Because your final negotiation will be within 5-10% of the first offer, in this case you will want to make the first ask. If you are really unsure of what the offer will be and want to play it safe, you can ask: *What is the budget you are working with?* at the moment that money becomes a discussion point.

Note: If you have yet to receive an offer and ask for an amount outside of your prospect's ballpark, this *could* jeopardize an offer. However, most people will simply say they can't (or won't) pay what you're asking and make a counter offer if they are interested.

2. **DON'T** apologize for what (e.g., money, benefits, or salary) you seek. If it is reasonable (and it should be), own it!

3. **DON'T** make the negotiation about economic need. Focus on your strengths, accomplishments, and results.

4. **DON'T** lie about your previous earnings or contracts. Answer truthfully and redirect the conversation back to the current opportunity and the main points of your argument.

5. **DON'T** take negotiations personally. Understand that every company operates differently and that the person hiring you may only have so much control.

A Final Pearl on Negotiations

The most successful negotiations are the ones where all parties involved have respect for one another's position AND have some chemistry and musicality in their communication. I'll never forget the first time I negotiated for a change in my job responsibilities. I was a pip squeak in college working for a nonprofit women's business development center. My direct supervisor had just given notice, and I was eager to take over one of her roles as newsletter editor. I knew that the executive director, with whom I'd be having the conversation with, loved a particular band. So I made sure to have their music playing in the office. Once the conversation began, I inserted a few jokes—one about the food at a recent fundraising event we'd just attended and another about her nemesis who had worn a horrible dress at a networking function we'd attended.

While the latter I would probably not do again for it was the epitome of cattie, although keep in mind I was nineteen, the important takeaway is that the strategy worked. I created an environment my executive director felt relaxed in. And I got someone who I was rather frightened of, to be perfectly honest, in the palm of my hand. I walked away with a new job title and a couple of extra dollars per hour to reflect it.

Finally, the most important principle is to be present to everything you say and do in a negotiation—from your phrasing to how you telegraph via your face. Take account of the impact it has on the party or parties you are speaking with. This way you can repeat what works, scrap what doesn't, and negotiate even more effectively next time. Also, the more adept you are at reading the body language of the people you are negotiating with, the more you will understand how to strengthen your verbal and *nonverbal* delivery.

From Offer to First Day

An offer may come at the end of an interview. Although more likely than not, it will come in a follow-up call or email, particularly if you are applying for a j-o-b. While it can feel like a salary or fee negotiation means that an offer is on the table, sometimes it is exactly what it is: a negotiation. **You don't have an offer until you have it in writing.** I say this not to scare you, and rather to remind you that you want an offer in writing even if it is initially made face-to-face or on the phone. This gives you the freedom to think about your response, give notice at a current job, send out an email blast to all of your friends and family, buy your celebratory pair of jeans or new suit, and start preparing for your first day.

Just as you expect a company or client to extend you a written offer, give them a formal, written "Yes," stating at a minimum the mutually agreed upon salary or fee, job title, start date, etc. If possible, ask for your benefits, key responsibilities and accountabilities to be spelled out and include them in your acceptance letter. Can you tell I like a paper trail?

If for any reason you choose to decline the opportunity, send or email a timely written response thanking the company or person (in the case of an individual client) for their time and consideration. Only state the reason that you are passing if it is based on a request you made and they couldn't honor (e.g., money, benefits, tuition-remission, etc.), and you want to make clear you hope they'll consider you in the future if *their* circumstances change.

SUCCESSwork: Ensuring Success Day 1

Okay, it is REALLY time to go hog wild and celebrate your offer! Give yourself a couple of days to honor all that you have done in your professional and personal development, the keen action steps you have taken, and the courage and faith you have consistently harnessed.

It can be so easy to ask, *"What's next?"* However, if we don't honor our achievements, particularly if they have been a long time coming, we are setting ourselves up for burnout. And although you may be coming to the end of one stage of success engineering, because CAREERpreneurship is a career-long process, you are actually gearing up to enter a new phase. And you want to show up to your first day at a new opportunity ready to shine!

Once you feel like you have done a little bit of celebration, relaxation, and renewal, full steam ahead with this final piece of SUCCESSwork… for the chapter.

Directions: Visualize yourself at the end of your first 90-days of this new opportunity. How have they unfolded?

What have you achieved?

_____

_____

_____

_____

Who have you been in and out of work?

_____

_____

_____

_____

What results have you achieved or are you moving towards?

_____

_____

_____

_____

What obstacles were you able to shift into possibilities for creative problem solving, collaboration, or delegation?

_____

_____

_____

_____

How is your new role contributing to your professional and personal learning and growth?

_____

_____

_____

_____

Now, begin to work backwards. Ask yourself this same set of questions for your first 60-days.

_____

_____

_____

_____

Go back another month and ask yourself where you were at the end of your first 30-days.

_____

_____

_____

_____

_____

Take yet another leap back to the end of your first week.

_____

_____

_____

_____

_____

And finally, go back to your first day.

_____

_____

_____

_____

_____

Now that you moved backwards from finish to start, go back through from start to finish. What goals and objectives are necessary to be _who_ and _where_ you want to be by the end of your first three months?

_____

_____

_____

_____

_____

Questions for Reflection

Identify for yourself: What choices in believing, thinking, and behaving enabled you to engineer success throughout your first 90-days in this new opportunity?

What kind of legacy will you ensure for yourself through each day of work and contribution?

How will you translate your discoveries into action?

Whether you worked through this chapter or just read it, your opportunities for success engineering continue long after landing a job or big client, even when it is your dream one. A cornerstone of being a CAREERpreneur is knowing that each day is an opportunity to align further your calling with your work.

While relishing the current moment, how can you still keep your eye on your two-steps ahead?

Chapter Fourteen

Positioning Myself as an Expert

While there are many lessons to learn from the recession that began in 2008, I believe one of the most important ones is to remember that even if your CAREERpreneur trajectory involves working full-time for one employer at a time, it is naïve to believe in job security. Unfortunately, NOBODY is immune from a lay-off, a business failure, a foreclosure, or a bankruptcy. It is vital to have your CAREERpreneurship mindset in place, your materials compiled, relationships built, and techniques (e.g., informational interviewing, engaging with online media, etc.) in practice so that you can be resilient in the face of any anticipated or unforeseen setback. And whether you are at the start of your CAREERpreneurship journey, nearing the final chapter, or more likely somewhere in between the two poles, you want to think about how to extend your name, reputation, and impact beyond the company or companies you are or will be working for, even if you are self-employed.

The first definition of an *expert* on Google, "having or showing knowledge and skills and aptitude," gets to the very heart of *who* an expert is. We all have a unique compilation of "knowledge and skills and aptitude." Those of us who know how to share it with the people who need it and will pay for it are those who are going reap the rewards of becoming an expert and make the greatest impact on our communities.

In this chapter, you are going to begin by envisioning yourself as an expert and then explore ways both to define your expertise and share it with those folks who can most benefit from it.

SUCCESSwork: Let's Welcome to the Stage, Expert _____ .

Directions: Imagine that you are nearing the end of your successful professional career. You are being honored for making an outstanding contribution in your field. Your colleagues, family, friends, and community have all been invited to participate in your tribute. A pioneer in your field, _____ , is about to read your Speech of Introduction.
(fill in the blank with a name)
Using the template below, create it.

Good evening. My name is _____ and
(fill in the blank with the name above)
it is with great pleasure that I welcome you to _____
(fill in the blank with the name of an event)
_____ to honor the incomparable _____ .
(fill in your name)
Over the last _____ years, _____
(fill in the blank with a number)   (fill in your name)
has accomplished such important and diverse achievements as
_____ to _____ . More
(fill in the blank with an achievement)   (fill in the blank with an achievement)
than anyone in the specific and important field of _____ ,
(fill in the blank with your field)
_____ knows _____ .
(fill in your name)   (fill in the blank with your expertise)
Those who have learned and grown from _____ , including
(fill in your name)
_____ and _____ ,
(fill in the blank with a name)   (fill in the blank with a name)
have described _____ impact as _____
(fill in your name)'s   (fill in the blank with a form of impact)
_____ , _____ ,
(fill in the blank with a form of impact)
and _____ . One admirer
(fill in the blank with a form of impact)
of _____ says that _____
(fill in the blank with a name)   (pick she or he)
knew just how significant _____ would be
(fill in your name)
when _____ . While
(fill in the blank with your name and an impact or achievement)
there are numerous accomplishments and accolades we could recognize
_____ for, what is perhaps most noteworthy is who
(fill in your name)
_____ has been in _____ relationships
(fill in your name)   (pick his or her)
with others. _____ shows up each day to life as someone
(fill in your name)
who _____ and _____ .
(fill in the blank with a quality)   (fill in the blank with a quality)
Please join me in welcoming to the stage _____ .
(fill in your name)

Questions for Reflection

How does it feel to imagine yourself being honored for your expertise?

How are you ensuring each day that you are working towards a legacy worthy of this speech and honor?

Through your expertise, what kind of impact have you been able to make on your local, national, and international community?

How has your life been enriched as a result of the contributions you have made?

Before we look at specific strategies for building your expertise and sharing it with the right audience, take note of the following materials you will want to start creating and compiling. And fortunately, about half of them you already possess! Those that you don't, I've put a star beside.

20 Things That Are Necessary to Be an "Expert"

1.   UBS
2.   15-30 Second Pitch
3.   Letter of Introduction
4.   Cover Letter
5.   Resume
6.   All-Star Team
7.   Testimonials
     They can live on your LinkedIn page, a website, or both (Include them with proposals or as references as appropriate)
8.   LinkedIn Profile
9.   Twitter Account
*10. A short-bio (1-paragraph) and a long-bio (2-3 paragraphs to 1 page)
*11. Facebook Fan Page—**Join *Alexia Vernon's Catalyst for Action* Fan Page!**
     Once you have a Facebook page, you can create a Fan Page and invite your existing friends to become fans. *(Revisit Chapter 10 for recommended privacy steps)*
*12. Business Card (separate from your job/company)
*13. Blog and/or Website (separate from your job/company)
*14. Headshot (for speaking and writing engagements as well as online profiles)
*15. A domain name that contains your name (e.g., http://www.AlexiaVernon.com)
     This will cost you about $10 each year and gives you access to free e-mail accounts.
*16. A professional email address (e.g., Alexia@AlexiaVernon.com)
     While Alexia.Vernon@gmail.com is all right, the above example (which is free after purchasing your domain name) is better.
*17. A FREE subscription to Help a Reporter Out ™

You will receive several emails each day where reporters and other media professionals request that experts on particular topics contact them to be cited in articles, books, radio and TV programs, etc. (I have both found experts and received media attribution through this service.)

*18. 1-3 adaptable 30-minute speeches/presentations

*19. 1-3 adaptable 1-3 hour workshops

*20. What Dan Schawbel refers to as a *personal press kit* or, if tailored toward speaking, a *speaker's one sheet*. Either document is a 1-page PDF file (can be front and back) that is placed on your website/blog for download and to be emailed; should contain the following:

A) A pleasing and easy to read design that reflects your brand

B) Your name and contact information

C) Your headshot

D) A brief bio (results-focused and incorporating your UBS)

E) Testimonials

F) A list of offerings and brief descriptions (e.g., keynotes, workshops, etc.)

G) Sample list of clients/experience

H) Sample list of previous media experience

Welcome to the Blogosphere

According to an article in *The Wall Street Journal* in 2009, the U.S. is a "nation of over 20 million bloggers, with 1.7 million profiting from the work, and 452,000 using blogging as their primary source of income." (As a point of reference, according to the Bureau of Labor Statistics as of this printing, the U.S. has 555,770 lawyers, 498,090 bartenders, and 394,710 computer programmers). eMarketer.com predicts that by 2012, more than 145 million people—or 67% of the U.S. Internet population—will be reading blogs at least once per month. So thinking of blogging as a fad is, well, a little like having said Beta would trump VHS…in other words, dead wrong!

My hope for you is not that you will make blogging a career, unless of course this is your passion. Rather, I want you to understand that blogging is an important AND easy way to share your expertise with others, connect with other experts (by commenting on their blogs, listing them in your Blogroll, and mentioning them in your posts), and set yourself up for desired and unforeseen opportunities. Over the last year, blogging has increasingly incorporated video uploads. Emerging and established experts can now vlog in lieu of or to augment their writing, making the medium even more accessible.

There are a number of easy to use blogging platforms. Blogger, the easiest platform to use and WordPress, which is just a bit more complex, are both FREE. (For $87 you can have the WordPress Thesis DIYtheme which lets you have a lot of freedom with design and use your blog template as a website.)

While there is no right way to create a blog, there are a number of best practices. They include:

1. Find a legitimate gap in the blogosphere and fill it.
2. Have a consistent domain name and title for your blog, either your name or a sticky phrase that captures the results readers can expect to achieve (Three of my favorite evocative blog titles (and blogs!) are Pamela Slim's *Escape from Cubicle Nation*, Kris Carr's *Crazy Sexy Life*, Andy Bellatti's *Small Bites*, and Deborah Siegel's, *Girl with Pen*.
3. Register your blog at Technorati.
4. Blog about a focused topic so that you can give in-depth information.
5. Post or vlog at least once per week.
6. Invite experts to submit guest posts or interview them for your blog. (This can help you achieve #5.)
7. Offer to be a guest blogger or interviewee for other bloggers.
8. Comment on other blogs.
9. Respond to people who post comments to your blog.
10. Whether blogging on your site or others, be honest, generous, and useful.

SUCCESSwork: Create Your Blog Profile

Directions: Before you do the rest of this SUCCESSwork, allocate a few hours over the next few days to surveying the blogosphere to see what blogs exist in your interest areas. Note what topics are popular, the angles they are covered from, and the openings that exist. An easy way to search recent blog topics is to go to the Google tool bar and under "more" select "Blogs." Then, enter specific words and phrases you want to explore.

After the step above, it's important to think through what you hope to achieve through blogging to design a blog that gets you what you are looking for. **Once you have surveyed the blogosphere and gotten a lay of the land, you can put together an overview of your blog by answering the following:**

1. People who read my blog are looking to…

    _____

    _____

    _____

2. A name for my blog that is sticky and reflects what readers will walk away with is….

    _____

    _____

    _____

3. 5 other blogs that my ideal reader goes to are…

    _____

    _____

    _____

4. My ideal reader will want to read my blog along with the blogs mentioned in #3 because…

_____

_____

_____

5. I would describe my ideal reader as…

_____

_____

_____

6. I will drive my ideal reader to my blog by…

_____

_____

_____

7. 8 topics (or 2 months of blog entries) could be about…

_____

_____

_____

8. My top 3 goals for my blog are…

_____

_____

_____

9. I will measure my blogging success by…

_____

_____

_____

10. In order to meet my blogging goals I must...

_____

_____

_____

Questions for Reflection

How does the blog you will create reflect the expertise you identified in your earlier Speech of Introduction SUCCESSwork from the chapter?

What role will blogging play in building and sharing your expertise?

What timeline is aggressive and achievable for launching your blog?

The Art of *The Offering*

I teach 4-8 hour workshops on presentations, yet I can scale EVERYTHING down to 2 questions you want to ask yourself anytime you set out to create one.

> *What do I want my participants to walk away with when I'm done?*
> *What do participants need to experience in order for that to happen?*

A successful presentation, whether it is a traditional 15-45 minute speech or a longer half or full-day workshop, has a basic outline. Rather than starting at the beginning and going through each phase, we will begin with the end in mind and work backwards to ensure that each step of your offering builds on the last to take your participants where you want them to go.

Call to Action: Participants know what they are supposed to do with the material you have shared. Usually, you want an audience to do one of the following:

1. Make a purchase (if you are doing a sales presentation)
2. Shift thinking or behavior (if you are persuading without selling a product or service)
3. Remember a new body of information (if you are teaching)

Conclusion: Before your call to action, participants have an opportunity to re-encounter your main points and the experience they took to get there. I'm a big believer in making conclusions interactive, even if that means you ask some questions like, *"What has been of most value for you today, and how will you put it into practice?"* and participants simply turn to one another for a minute to share their answers.

Body: In the heart of your speech or workshop, participants are exposed to 3 key ideas. There are a variety of formats you might use depending on your purpose. **If you are seeking to sell something**, you must answer: *Why you? Why this product or service?*

Why now? **If you are looking to shift thinking or behavior**, you typically will want to identify the problem with what people are doing, explain the cause, and then provide the solution. **If you are trying to communicate new information**, you want to identify about three main points related to your specific purpose and spend equal time covering each of them. **When leading a workshop**, you are likely engaged in skill or knowledge development. In this instance, your goal is to provide ample opportunities to collect and try out this information by covering your key points and then letting participants get up on their feet and put it into action.

Introduction: After briefly introducing yourself (and if in a group, letting participants get to know one another), **you want to grab everyone's attention, reveal the topic of the presentation or workshop, provide evidence of your credibility, and let them know what they will walk away with by the end.**

10 Ways to Ensure Your Offering Gets Your Target Market Saying *Wow*

1. Speak *with* rather than *at* participants and connect with them in the head (intellectually), heart (emotionally), and gut (bodily and instinctually).
2. Give participants what they *want* so that you can give them what they *need.* (While you may have an agenda, ensure that you are promoting what will get people in the door and engaged first.)
3. Use humor often and never at anyone's expense.
4. Find opportunities for participant engagement beyond a Q and A at the end.
5. Use visual aids to help an audience understand and imagine information (e.g., pictures, graphs, comics, etc.) and not to communicate your points (e.g., paragraphs, too many bullet points, or a lot of text that simply repeats what you are saying).
6. Tell relevant stories throughout.
7. Rehearse, Rehearse, Rehearse (When you "wing it" you waste everyone's time.)

8. Dress appropriately for the occasion. (Have one piece of clothing or accessory pop.)

9. Customize your offering for each group of participants.

10. Give participants an opportunity to explore how they will translate what they have encountered into action.

SUCCESSwork: Creating the Skeleton of Your Offering

Directions: In a journal or on your computer, take what you have learned about your expertise from your first two sets of SUCCESSwork for the chapter and outline a speech or workshop from your Call to Action backwards through to your Introduction. Focus on your main points for each section and note sub-points, activities, examples, stories, jokes, and other ideas that pop up as you go through your initial design. Afterwards, answer these questions.

1. What is a sticky title for your offering?

    _____

    _____

    _____

    _____

    _____

2. What is a 3-5 sentence description of your offering?

    _____

    _____

    _____

_____

_____

3. What are 3-5 things participants will take away from the offering?

_____

_____

_____

_____

_____

4. What will you say to prospective participants who don't "get" the need for your offering?

_____

_____

_____

_____

_____

5. What 5 anecdotal and statistical sources can you cite to give validity to your offering?

_____

_____

_____

_____

_____

Questions for Reflection

Who would be most interested in your offering AND willing to give you what you desire? (e.g., a speaker's fee, purchase a product you might be selling, offer you a job, book you for another event, mention you in their press, etc.)

Where will you find these people? (e.g., local networking group, professional association, civic organization, nonprofit, university or school department, industry conference, etc.)

How will you present your offering to the people in the reflection question above so that it is irresistibly attractive to them? How will you answer: *Why you? Why the topic? Why now?*

What will be the professional and personal payoff for preparing and presenting this offering?

There is A LOT of information to process and many opportunities for professional development contained in this chapter. While there is no time like the present to dive in and start building and sharing your expertise, be kind to yourself and don't expect to make it all happen before Chapter 15. Continue to revisit this SUCCESSwork so that as you're finding the next evolutions of your brand of CAREERpreneurship, you remember that you have the tools and expertise to think and live bigger. You just need to harness the courage, allocate the time, and connect with the people to make it happen!

Chapter Fifteen

A Lesson from Octopuses

We will kick off our second to last chapter together by exploring a cornerstone of success engineering—*praxis*. The notion of praxis comes from the Brazilian educational philosopher, Paulo Freire, who believed that too often human beings get stymied in their thinking. He believed that it is vital for us to take *action*, *reflect* upon it, and then take new action based upon the reflection, which he calls *transformation*. Praxis is not a linear process. Instead it's a continuous one of balancing smart action with reflection and then new, more informed action.

I see the praxis process as being like an octopus. You want to have your tentacles out at all times, pulling in possibilities for success as well as feedback on how you are doing, so that you can keep stepping up your game and engineering new levels of achievement. Now, a lot of your SUCCESSwork has asked you to assess your strengths and areas for growth. It is also important to solicit and be open to outside feedback.

What is Feedback?

In coaching, feedback is the practice of honoring specific successful practices in thinking, believing, and behaving while providing or receiving coachee-centered recommendations for improving performance in each of these areas. In order for feedback to be "coachee-centered," it's important for the person giving the feedback to have the recipient's trust and permission, be enough of an expert to offer useful and accurate perceptions and recommendations, make feedback about skills and behaviors rather than personality characteristics, keep suggestions action-oriented, link recommendations to short and long-term goals, and not be attached to the outcome of the coachee's performance. While this last requirement is often impossible to achieve in workplace coaching—hence the demand for external coaches—it should be adhered to whenever you give and receive feedback on one's CAREERpreneurship practice, such as in the following SUCCESSwork.

SUCCESSwork: Becoming a *Sensei* of Feedback

In Japanese culture, the title of sensei is given as a show of respect to someone who has achieved mastery in a field. Regardless of your professional background, you want to be a sensei of feedback. The more "good" feedback we give and receive, the better able we are to make smart choices, self-correct our not such good ones, and be of service to others.

Directions: Identify an area of CAREERpreneurship that feels a little wonky for you. Perhaps you are not entirely pleased with your Paragraph of Introduction or you feel like your interviewing persona comes across as inauthentic. **Identify a member of your All-Star Team or perhaps reach out to another reader on Twitter via #CAREERpreneur and ask for some feedback.**

Make sure that whomever you ask meets the criteria we have just discussed—most importantly that the person is without agenda and can keep recommendations skill and behavior based. Give the person a brief overview of what you would like feedback on, how you hope to benefit from it, and its relevance to your short and long-term goals. Then, ask the person to address the following.

1) What specifically do you feel like I'm doing well?
2) What are you basing this assessment on?
3) In what areas do you feel like I have room for growth?
4) What are you basing that assessment on?

5) What recommendations can you offer for how to increase my success in
_____ area?

6) Is there anything else I should know to help me reach my full potential
in this area?

Now, because you also learn and grow from *giving* feedback, identify someone in
your professional or personal life who could benefit from feedback around one of
your strengths. It could be something you have mastered in this program or a strength
you came in with. In either circumstance, let the person identify clearly for you what
she or he wants to focus on, what she or he has been doing in the feedback area, how
it connects to her or his short and long-term goals, and how she or he hopes to grow
from the feedback. Then, launch into the feedback questions.

Questions for Reflection

What have you discovered both from giving and receiving feedback?

How close were your perceptions to those of the person or people you spoke with?

How are you translating what you have learned about yourself into action?

What Happens When I Get in a Rut?

I get asked this question all the time from clients in their third to fourth month of coaching. Once someone identifies that trying new ways of thinking, believing, and doing can unlock possibilities and catalyze learning and growth, solidifying the new habits to sustain success often comes quickly. Sure, we have a few hiccups along the way. But after a few weeks in, we see the changes in *who* we are and get better at keeping ourselves on course.

And then, as I mentioned a moment ago, we get just past the habit stage. We no longer have to direct as much energy and attention to our beliefs, thoughts, or behaviors which on the surface sounds pretty great; however, it also means that if we get thrown for a curve ball (e.g., we lose a job, break-up with a partner, or even just feel down because of a change in weather), we are no longer as committed to staying the course. The key here is not to think the habit isn't there or we are bad or unworthy, or engage in any other thinking that will trigger a spiral downward.

What do you do if you forget to make the bed? Or brush your teeth at night? My suspicion is you make note of it and self-correct the next day. And these are habits too, yes?

The next time you find yourself conceding to old limiting beliefs or habits, revert back to one of the exercises in your next SUCCESSwork. To get them in your bones, try them this week, no matter how successful you are feeling as a CAREERpreneur. I don't think it's possible to have too robust of a personal foundation!

SUCCESSwork: The Perpetual Optimist's Essential Tools

Directions: Complete each of the following exercises, and consider how to best incorporate them into your ongoing personal foundation work.

1.   **The Glad Game**
     Remember the Disney classic, *Pollyanna*? The titular character is a young orphan who goes to live with her miserly Aunt Polly in Vermont after her parents'

untimely death. She transforms her aunt's dispirited town with "The Glad Game." Anytime she or her neighbors give in to idle gossip, whining, or sadness, Pollyanna challenges them to cite one thing that makes them glad. And in no time, even ole Aunt Polly can't help but count her blessings.

Directions: Spend the next 5 minutes having a stream-of-consciousness brainstorm, beginning with the phrase, "I'm glad about..." Let one source of gladness lead, without analysis, into the next. (e.g., I'm glad about this sunny morning, the book I'm reading, my new haircut, that I am caught up on email, that I no longer have to eat my mother's brussels sprouts, etc.)

2.   **Harness Your *Chutzpah***

Roxanne Ravenel, a job search coach and consultant, says (and I concur) that audacity is an important skill for climbing from your calling to your career.

> *"Successful job hunters possess moxie, boldness. They are willing to put themselves out there to a certain degree. Ann Ronan, who landed her dream job as a health educator did just that. She wanted to be a health educator. She found the company she wanted to work for, went into their office and announced, "I really want to work here." They found a volunteer opportunity for her. Later she transitioned to a paid position."*

While I refer to audacity as *chutzpah*, for I think saying the Yiddish word is the very epitome of acting courageously, the sentiment is the same.

This week identify one thing to pursue EACH day that pushes you outside of your comfort zone, can further your learning and growth, and do it! Pay particular attention to how you feel just after pushing through the scary space. Here are five ideas you may consider:

1.   Initiate a conversation with a stranger.
2.   Admit you don't have the answer to something you are supposed to know.

3. Wear an article of clothing that attracts attention.

4. Apologize for something you have not taken accountability for.

5. Figure out how much you want to make each year, and then tell five people how you plan to make it happen.

3. **The Not-So-Random Act of Kindness**

Ever since Oprah started discussing Random Acts of Kindness on her show, everyone from positive psychologists to self-help junkies have championed the idea of going out and doing something unexpected and kind for others, often times strangers. While it is great to give people pleasant surprises, it is even greater to give people what they want and don't have.

Directions: Identify someone you know who has a need that isn't being filled. Give the person something that will make a positive impact. I've included five examples clients and I have done before to trigger ideas.

1. Cook and deliver a meal to someone who doesn't have enough time to spend with family.

2. Play babysitter to someone who needs some time away from his or her children.

3. Hold someone accountable to her or his goals.

4. Be a workout buddy.

5. Help someone plant a garden, clear out a closet, or weed out other home clutter.

Questions for Reflection

What is the impact of redirecting your attention back to what is working in your life (and in the world)?

Who would you have to be to let courage and love (rather than fear) motivate ALL of your choices?

How does investing in yourself and others promote a myriad of benefits? (e.g., social, emotional, spiritual, etc.)

We often think that it is our big disappointments or setbacks that have the greatest negative impact on our life satisfaction. And while I'm certainly not going to "poo poo" the devastation we feel after a job loss, break-up, cross-country move, or the death of a loved one (situations you have most likely gone through, just like me), I am going to remind you that most of us bounce back to how we felt prior to the negative incident shortly thereafter. On the flipside, it's often our tolerations (*which we explored in Chapter 2*) and negative interpretations of our experiences (e.g., If it snows for a fourth day in a row I'm going to pack up and move to a tropical island or I'm never going to have enough money to live the life I want.) that we allow to frustrate us to no end and sour our worldview. This is why staying committed to personal foundation work is one of the most important practices for a CAREERpreneur.

When we find ourselves in this kind of an unproductive mental place, life coach Christine Hassler, who is the author of the books, *The 20 Something Manifesto* and *20-Something, 20-Everything: A Quarter-life Woman's Guide to Balance and Direction*, recommends listening to that message that is underneath that drizzle of persistent complaint or the source of *"the funk."* She says, *"You can do this by asking yourself questions such as, 'Is there a way I am not taking care of my own needs? Am I out of integrity with myself or another in some way? Is there unfinished business or an incomplete conversation lingering about? Have I been in my head a lot and perhaps ignoring my feelings? Am I overly focused on another or an external situation?'"* Then, Hassler says, *"You can go into the inquiry of the funk by just allowing yourself to free form write or talk aloud."* When we're dialogical with our negative self-talk, we often allow our needed answers to emerge. We can identify a solution and shift back into a more desired way of thinking, feeling, and behaving.

To close the chapter, I'm going to ask you to complete some SUCCESSwork that supports you in remembering all of the tools you have amassed and begun to play with throughout the book to connect your personal growth with success engineering.

SUCCESSwork: Seeking an Experienced Director of Sustainable Life Satisfaction

Directions: Imagine that you are interested in applying for the following job opportunity:

WANTED: An experienced Director of Sustainable Life Satisfaction for Happiness, Inc. We invite CAREERpreneurs from across disciplines that know how to engineer sustainable life satisfaction to apply. Please submit a cover letter and resume explaining why you are the best candidate for this position.

Using everything you have learned about building a strong personal foundation, creating and sharing an authentic brand, and crafting an employer-centered cover letter, type or write in a journal your Cover Letter for the position.

Questions for Reflection
What do you "know" about engineering sustainable life satisfaction?

How much are you walking the walk through your daily choices in thinking, feeling, and behaving?

What opportunities are you committed to pursuing in order to be a model to everyone in your life (e.g., employers, colleagues, friends, and family) of optimum life satisfaction?

Chapter Sixteen

Crossing the Finish Line

Before your break open a bottle of champagne, sparkling apple cider, or some other bubbly drink of choice to celebrate the completion of this first phase of your CAREERpreneurship journey, you have some final SUCCESSwork. (Although your previous SUCCESSwork <u>can</u> and <u>should</u> be revisited to continue climbing from your calling to your career!) Yes, it's time to create your own 16-weeks (or Phase II) of *Awaken Your CAREERpreneur.*

SUCCESSwork: Designing Phase II

Directions: As you did in Chapter 13, I'm going to ask you to visualize yourself a few months from now, in this case 4-months or 16-weeks forward.

What have you achieved?

_____

_____

_____

_____

_____

Who have you been professionally and personally?

_____

_____

_____

_____

_____

What results have you achieved or are you moving towards?

_____

_____

_____

_____

What obstacles were you able to shift into possibilities for creative problem solving, collaboration, or delegation?

_____

_____

_____

_____

How have you furthered your learning, growth, and success?

_____

_____

_____

_____

Now, begin to work backwards. Ask yourself this same set of questions for your first 90-days post Phase I of *Awaken Your CAREERpreneur.*

_____

_____

_____

_____

_____

Go back another month and ask yourself where you were at the end of your first 60-days?

_____

_____

_____

_____

Where were you at the end of your first 30-days?

_____

_____

_____

_____

Take yet another leap back to the end of your first week. Where were you?

_____

_____

_____

_____

_____

And finally, go back to your first day.

_____

_____

_____

_____

Now that you have moved backwards from finish to start, go back through from start to finish.

What goals and objectives are necessary to be _who_ and _where_ you want to be in the next 4-months? How will you design your own CAREERpreneurship program and accompanying SUCCESSwork to get you there?

_____

_____

_____

_____

To ensure that you are able to convert your musings into results-oriented action, let's take a look at how to create a SMART 120-Day Plan.

SMART Plans Are...

Specific: The more CAREERpreneurs define exactly *what* they are expecting to do, *who* is involved, and *who* they are expecting to be, the more they set themselves up to succeed. They should consider anticipated and unforeseen obstacles to goal achievement and ensure that they are designing action items that shift these possible challenges into strategies for troubleshooting, learning, and growing. Also, CAREERpreneurs want to keep themselves open to opportunities (the good, the bad, and the confusing) that the universe sends their way and that they didn't anticipate. How will *you* push yourself to capitalize on the success that is your birthright without getting too locked into the structure you create for yourself?

Measurable: Every goal needs clear, specific criteria for evaluation. What will success be based on? What are the *different* ways you can be successful? CAREERpreneurs want specific dates assigned for key benchmarks and weekly action items so that success can be achieved throughout the journey and not just upon arriving at the destination. Also, consider how *you* will check-in along the way to adjust your expectations and timeline based on the possibilities the universe sends your way.

Achievable: Goals should be something that CAREERpreneurs can accomplish based on their time, ability, effort, and resources. They should be able to control their efficacy and not need to rely too heavily on other people or unpredictable circumstances for goal fulfillment. How will *you* ensure that you can fulfill the goals you set for yourself?

Relevant: Goals should be based on alignment between values, strengths, resources, and enthusiasms. As a CAREERpreneur, *you* should know clearly the purpose for undertaking the goal at this particular time and the short and long-term benefits for achieving it.

Timely: To stay motivated, feel a sense of accomplishment, and evaluate effort and achievement appropriately, CAREERpreneurs should be able to accomplish goals in 120-days or less with measurable action items fleshed out for each week. *You* can dissect long-term goals into a series of interconnected SMART goals.

Using these SMART guidelines, create *your* individualized 4-month plan!

Awaken Your CAREERpreneur **PHASE II:**
My Next 4-Months

Goals: (List up to 3)

1. To...

2. To...

3. To...

Indicators of Success (List for each goal)

1.

2.

3.

Professional and Personal Payoff (List for each goal)

1.

2.

3.

<u>Action Steps</u>   <u>Dates for Completion</u>

(Use your reflections at the start of the SUCCESSwork to make sure that where you are starting today and each action you take afterwards leads you SMART-ly toward your intended destination).

1.

2.

3.

4.

5.

6.

7.

8.

9.

10.

SUCCESSwork Assignments   Action Step(s) Attached To

1.

2.

3.

4.

5.

Possible Obstacles   Strategies for Troubleshooting

1.

2.

3.

4.

5.

As a reminder, after embarking on a SMART Plan, it's important to adjust action items and quite possibly the goal in lieu of discoveries made along the way. As anyone who has embarked on a road trip knows, there are usually half a dozen ways to get from where you are starting to where you want to be going. As you get in the car and start driving, you often discover that the seemingly shortest path has the most treacherous terrain, or construction you didn't anticipate, or a fabulous back road you couldn't help but follow. Other times you've been driving for hours thinking you are on the right freeway only to discover you made a wrong turn somewhere along the way and are now utterly lost. A SMART Plan should not be a static road map; rather, it should function like a GPS. It illuminates the range of possibilities for success. As a CAREERpreneur, you do some initial planning, get on the road, and know that you can adjust your route at any time, no matter how behind schedule or lost you may at times feel.

Although I never questioned the destination I set for myself when choosing to become a career and leadership coach, less than a year into my business, I felt like my road map was a little wonky. After half a dozen marketing and business building workshops and webinars, I decided I would focus my practice around creatives (e.g., actors, dancers, musicians, visual artists, etc.) and nonprofit professionals (e.g., administrators, educators, social workers, youth development practitioners, etc.). These were the people I felt I could most relate to for their backgrounds best reflected my own. While my intentions were certainly pure and logical, what I could only learn from getting out in the trenches, sharing what I did with my "ideal clients," and ultimately coaching them was that I often fell more into the role of consultant than coach. People came to me because of my expertise in their career fields. As a result, rather than empowering them to find their own best answers to their curiosities and concerns which lay within themselves all along, I started telling them what I thought. While skilled coaches certainly can share our perceptions, particularly if and when we have intuitive responses, we should be doing about 80% of the *listening* and 20% of the *talking*. It took working with a mentor coach and partnering with a few clients who were in such unfamiliar fields as finance and publishing for me to recognize I needed and wanted to get back to coaching. I also needed and wanted to watch my tendency to collapse into consulting, redefine my ideal client (I chose to focus on folks who wanted to engage in holistic leadership and career development rather than on people in a particular industry), and most importantly, keep trudging ahead and applying the principles of praxis (*as we explored in Chapter 15*) to my brand of CAREERpreneurship.

Now, before *you* set off to activate your road map for the next 4-months (which, as you can see, is just a guide and not a prescription), take this opportunity to engage in some reflection around this milestone you have just hit, completing Phase I of the book.

SUCCESSwork: *Awaken Your CAREERpreneur*
Culminating Reflection

Directions: As you have done in previous chapters, bring yourself back to that physical environment where whole body reflection can take place. Make sure that the following questions and your answers to previous SUC-CESSwork are in tow. Take some time to release any tension you might be holding in your body. Bring your awareness to your breath, and take some nice, deep inhalations and exhalations. Once you have had some delicious moments of relaxation, muse on the following questions. Record your answers so that you can continue to track and celebrate your progress!

1. What are the Top 3 ways you have strengthened your personal foundation through reading the book and completing the SUCCESSwork?

    _____

    _____

    _____

    _____

    _____

2. What are the Top 3 things you have learned over the last 8 chapters in *The CAREERpreneur's Essential Tools?*

_____

_____

_____

_____

_____

3. What are the Top 3 things you have learned about CAREERpreneurship throughout the book?

_____

_____

_____

_____

_____

4. Where is there some additional room for learning and growth?

_____

_____

_____

_____

5. How has your professional vision of *who* you want to be, *what* you want to be doing, and *how* you will be showing up to opportunities evolved?

_____

_____

_____

_____

_____

6. How will you continue to apply the principles you have learned as you move into Phase II of *Awaken Your CAREERpreneur* and throughout the rest of your career?

_____

_____

_____

_____

_____

> *What is success? To laugh often and much and to win the respect of intelligent people and the affection of children; to earn the appreciation of honest critics and endure the betrayal of false friends; to appreciate beauty, to find the best in others, to leave the world a bit better, whether by a healthy child, a garden patch or a redeemed social condition; to know even one life has breathed easier because you have lived; this is to have succeeded.* (Ralph Waldo Emerson)

There is not a doubt in my mind that you will keep harnessing your values, strengths, resources, and enthusiasms to lead people toward social, economic, and environmental solutions that are for the greater good, derive peak life satisfaction for your energy and efforts, and cultivate a legacy you can be proud of. Continue to show up to each day of your life at 100% so that you can play at 100%. And know that even in those inevitable professional and personal dark moments—the ones where you feel like someone has taken a machete and scooped out your heart, your confidence, or your faith—that these too are opportunities for something magical. They're usually our biggest opportunities, and they come our way when we're ready to discover new reservoirs of our strength, our resilience, and our truth. As a CAREERpreneur, we are charged to say thank you when they find us, give ourselves permission to feel the pain, reflect upon it, and then use our insight and commitment to fulfilling our potential to bulldoze forward and get back to the provocative work we have been called to do. You were put on this earth for greatness. It's your responsibility to make it happen.

It has been a privilege taking this journey with you. As a THANK YOU for believing that success is your birthright and choosing me as a partner in the process, I'd like to offer you a **SPECIAL GIFT**.

****FREE SUCCESS STRATEGY SESSION****

Presented to: _____
(Insert Your Name)

Presented by: Alexia@AwakenYourCareerpreneur.com

*To redeem your COMPLIMENTARY 15-minute Success Strategy Session,
kindly email me at Alexia@AwakenYourCareerpreneur.com with the
Top 3 Things you have discovered by reading the book and
your contact information.

Now, go activate your 4-Month Plan and open that bottle to celebrate your success! You most certainly deserve it.

Yours in sustainable success,

Coach Alexia

Acknowledgements

I am who I am and my work is what it is because of the unconditional love of my family and friends. To Mom, Steve, and Allen, thank you for sharing this ride most intimately with me, for listening to me as I talked through ideas, and for showing me that home is wherever you are. To Dad and Aunt Elaine, thank you for honoring my voice from across state lines and for being two of my biggest cheerleaders. Much aloha to you both. Sarah Morey, Kiran Rikhye, and Jon Stancato, my dear friends who have housed, fed, and shared so much laughter and more than a few tears with me as I've juggled working on two coasts (well, a coast and a desert), I'm eternally grateful. Nicole McDermet and Shauna Perry, my Forest Ridge sisters and oldest bosom buddies, thank you for knowing when to listen, when to advise, and when to bust out an inappropriate joke.

To my many mentors, particularly Mitalene Fletcher, Alexandra Lopez, Chris Vine, Helen White, and the rest of my CAT family, you always gave me the right balance of structure and freedom to do the best possible work and to do it with my own voice. Thank you. Jille Bartolome, you have been so much more than a teacher and a mentor. Every developing coach should be required to partner with you! And of course to Gabby Bernstein, thank you for your inspiration, guidance, and for helping me navigate my way through the publishing world and to approach all of my choices with love rather than fear. You have most definitely turned my ~ing on.

To my colleagues and clients, thank you for helping me walk the walk and for pushing me to have the courage and faith to take my message to a bigger audience. A special shout out goes to my chief proselytizers Andy Bellatti, Suzanne Grossman, Bethany Lahammer, Theresa Leavens, Shannon MacIntyre, and Selena Soo. Thank you to ASTD-Las Vegas and the Nevada Professional Coaches Association (NPCA) for believing in my ability to serve and to Wende Jager-Hyman, Becca Marcus, and the many *fierce* ladies at the Woodhull Institute for Ethical Leadership for giving me the opportunity to share my voice on and off the page.

A very special thank you to Natalie Gratkowski, intern extraordinaire. Your energy and enthusiasm to this project can be felt in every page.

To John Paul Owles and the rest of my Joshua Tree Publishing team, thank you for letting my vision guide every step of this project and for believing in the power of CAREERpreneurship. And Mindy Miller, thank you for getting up at 4AM and taking me out to another crazy location to shoot beautiful pictures while I flailed around like a rebellious monkey.

Much thanks also goes out to the fabulous CAREERpreneurs who contributed their wisdom and personal stories to inspire others to engineer their version of professional and personal success. May you and the next generation of CAREERpreneurs keep spreading your powerful message and shifting the way we go about charting our careers.

About the Author

Alexia Vernon

Career, Leadership, and Generations Expert
Author * Speaker * ICF Certified Coach * Trainer

Alexia Vernon is the owner of Catalyst for Action, a coaching and training company that empowers leaders to build careers and companies that achieve the 3 S's: success, sustainability, and a positive social impact. Alexia draws on her background as an actor and dancer to facilitate interactive, participant-centered learning opportunities for companies, colleges, professional associations, and community groups in such areas as career development, intergenerational and values-driven leadership, coaching for managers, effective interpersonal communication and public speaking, and women's empowerment. Each year Alexia reaches thousands of executives, managers, professionals, educators and students through her offerings and has worked with a range of organizations including the National Association of REALTORS® (NAR), the New York City Department of Education (DOE), National Council for Workforce Education (NCWE), American Society for Training and Development (ASTD), International Executive Housekeepers Association (IEHA), Step Up Women's Network, Net Impact, College Summit, Woodhull Institute for Ethical Leadership, Women Entrepreneurs (WE) and such colleges as The City University of New York (CUNY), Wells College, St. John's College, Manhattan College, Washington State University, West Virginia State University, DeVry University, College of Southern Nevada (CSN), and New Jersey City University.

Alexia has been featured in and contributed to myriad media, such as *The Wall Street Journal*, *Diversity Executive*, *New Jersey Monthly*, *Backstage Weekly*, FabJob.com's *Become a Career Coach*, MainStreet.com, Brand Camp University, CollegeRecruiter.com, TheGlassHammer.com, InternAdvocate.com, and Gradspot.com. Her blog, *Musings from the Generation We Coach*, is on Blogs.com's "Top 10 Blogs to Read If You've Just Been Laid Off.

Awaken Your CAREERpreneur

A HOLISTIC ROAD MAP TO CLIMB FROM YOUR CALLING TO YOUR CAREER

To join the *Awaken Your CAREERpreneur* community, read the blog, and stay abreast of CAREERpreneur seminars and events, visit

http://www.AwakenYourCareerpreneur.com

To contact Alexia to inquire about coaching and training solutions for you or your company, university, community organization, professional association, or to have her speak at your next event, email

Alexia@AwakenYourCareerpreneur.com

To learn more about Alexia Vernon and her company, Catalyst for Action, visit

http://www.AlexiaVernon.com

LaVergne, TN USA
19 September 2010
197527LV00003B/2/P